PROJECT BASED
LEARNING

PROJECT BASED LEARNING

Real Questions. Real Answers.
How to Unpack PBL and Inquiry

Ross Cooper AND **Erin Murphy**

Project Based Learning
© 2021 by Times 10 Publications

These books are available at special discounts when purchased in quantity for premiums, promotions, fundraising, and educational use. For inquiries and details, contact us at 10Publications.com.

Published by Times 10
Highland Heights, OH
10Publications.com

Cover and Interior Design by Steven Plummer
Editing by Carrie White-Parrish
Copyediting by Jennifer Jas

Library of Congress Cataloging-in-Publication Data is available.

Hardcover ISBN: 978-1-948212-27-4
Paperback ISBN: 978-1-948212-25-0
eBook ISBN: 978-1-948212-61-8

First Printing: March, 2021

Praise for Project Based Learning

None of us enjoy being taught at, and yet that is what too many students endure in their classroom. *Project Based Learning: Real Questions. Real Answers. How to Unpack PBL and Inquiry* is an inspiring book focusing on a process where the teacher and students learn together, and the authors provide a step-by-step process on how to do that.

— PETER DeWITT, EdD, AUTHOR, CONSULTANT, FINDING
COMMON GROUND BLOG FOR EDUCATION WEEK

This book is a must-read for educators who aspire to create more personalized and inquiry-based experiences for all students. Too often the message is that you have to start from scratch. Instead, Cooper and Murphy share insights and practical strategies to address the most pressing questions about project based learning and will empower you to build from what you are already doing to create amazing learning opportunities for your students.

— KATIE MARTIN, PhD, CHIEF IMPACT OFFICER AT ALTITUDE
LEARNING, AUTHOR OF *LEARNER-CENTERED INNOVATION*

The authors provide educators with the keys to deliver the type of learning all students deserve: engaging, hands-on, and on the path to caring about and solving problems that matter. As someone who facilitates project based learning with students, I'll be referring to this book, over and over again.

— SHELLY SANCHEZ, DIGITAL INNOVATOR, STEM TEACHER,
AUTHOR OF *HACKING DIGITAL LEARNING STRATEGIES*

Students around the world eagerly embrace learning experiences that are DIFFERENT, that are more than traditional factual recall and procedural regurgitation. In this phenomenal PBL resource, Cooper and Murphy unpack the concrete logistics of what it takes to facilitate deeper learning, greater student agency, and more real-world authentic work in your school. This book is full of useful templates and protocols, answers to challenging questions, and ideas that will energize student learning. Use the practical strategies in this book to embrace the "productive struggle" and make learning different (Please? Asking for a few million students …).

— SCOTT McLEOD, PhD, ASSOCIATE PROFESSOR, UNIVERSITY OF
COLORADO DENVER, FOUNDING DIRECTOR OF CASTLE

Ross Cooper and Erin Murphy have created a project based learning manifesto. One that can be read cover-to-cover or used over and over again as a PBL manual as questions naturally arise during the process. Created by two practitioners currently working in schools, the authors weave stories in and out of step-by-step strategies to make PBL doable, relevant, and meaningful. Get this book, and then get some highlighters and sticky notes because you are going to need them!

— A.J. Juliani, Coauthor of *Empower* and *LAUNCH*

Cooper and Murphy have created a guide for educators that answers questions around project based learning with steps readers can take to make PBL come to life in their classrooms. This book includes examples that can help you envision PBL in action along with plenty of resources to help you dive deeper into a PBL experience. If you've considered trying out project based learning with students or are ready to strengthen this practice, this book is for you!

— Monica Burns, EdD, Author of *Tasks Before Apps*, Founder of ClassTechTips.com

If you are an educator (or educational leader) who centers students, inquiry, and self-directed learning, then this is the book for you. Ross Cooper and Erin Murphy have created a thoughtful project based learning roadmap that helps educators understand how PBL can be a framework for all content areas so we no longer have to schedule PBL time as a stand-alone experience. Rich with graphics and organizers, *Project Based Learning: Real Questions. Real Answers. How to Unpack PBL and Inquiry* is a powerful resource that helps demystify PBL and makes it accessible to all teachers and learners with practical strategies and transformative resources!

— Tony Sinanis, EdD, 2014 NYS Elementary Principal of the Year, Coauthor of *Hacking Leadership*

For all the educators who put students at the center of their work. For all the administrators who leverage their title to elevate others.

—Ross

For all the learners who deserve to know and be known.

—Erin

Table of Contents

Foreword

B EFORE YOU TURN the page, I'm going to ask you to take some time to reflect on *your own* school experience. Whether it was a few years ago, or a few decades ago, what are those learning experiences that you remember most? What were those experiences that kept you most engaged? Which experiences had the best deeper learning outcomes? What experiences worked to build the skills you'd use after graduation? Which learning experiences put *you* at the center? Why? How?

Today's "Netflix Generation" of learners is more diverse than any in history. Simultaneously, a connected student today has more information in the palm of her hand than could be consumed in many lifetimes. In some classrooms, learning experiences remain focused on control, compliance, and conformity; while in others, problem-solving, creation, and deeper learning are part of the everyday experience. Twenty-first century tools are layered on top of twentieth century pedagogy in some settings; while in others, future ready skills are developed, and students are prepared for whatever it is they choose to do after high school. In some places, the mandated experience schools the love of learning right out of a child by the time he graduates. In others, a passion to change the world is ignited and the obtained skills make it possible.

Which type of classroom, school, or district do you lead? How do you know?

When you *know your why* for innovation, project based learning (PBL) is one of your best tools for your instructional toolbox.

When you commit to your why, *the how* comes into focus, and this book is going to be an incredible resource to propel your journey forward.

It's hard to argue that the regurgitation of low-level material, averaged together over time to determine learning outcomes, is even remotely relevant, nor does it adequately prepare learners for life ahead. More innovative approaches are needed to remain relevant for this generation of learners. In designing innovative experiences grounded in deep instructional methodologies, we can make the learning experience both *modern and meaningful*. When filled with agency and empathy, and empowered by dynamic real-world skills, today's learners can undoubtedly change the world around them. It's no secret that they already are.

During the global coronavirus pandemic, seventeen-year-old Avi Schiffmann of Seattle designed and coded *nCov2019.live*, an up-to-the-minute website accessed by millions of people per day that provides statistics on the number of confirmed COVID-19 cases around the world. His purpose? Providing people access to accurate information while keeping their anxiety in check. Although his grades may not be what others would deem successful, his impact is profound.

Having seen the impact of Hurricane Harvey firsthand, thirteen-year-old Sir Darius Brown of New Jersey set out on a mission to learn to sew bow ties for cats and dogs to help them get adopted. He didn't have much money, but he was filled with creativity and a deep sense of purpose. He designed and created five hundred bow ties that have been used to help animals all over the world.

Yet, it shouldn't take a disaster for students to have opportunities to design, create, follow their passions, or have an opportunity to display empathy. Nor should these breakthroughs only happen outside of school.

In Oakland, California, tenth graders in their Intro to Education class learned about literature by creating their own children's books for a village in Burkina Faso, a country in West Africa, where a school was being built. The students didn't *begin* by studying children's literature. They found an authentic audience and published unique pieces for them.

Relevance and purpose are essential components of project based learning. It's why some of the greatest experiences for students are found in solving problems close to home.

Kindergarten students visiting the local animal shelter during their animal unit and working collaboratively to put together community signs to promote adoption. Third graders interviewing students about the current school snack availability in an effort to create a campaign around healthy eating. Fifth graders writing letters to their local township and proposing plans for better and more efficient recycling in their community. The possibilities for your classroom, and more importantly, *your students' impact*, are endless.

Project based learning utilizes a learner-centered lens, and ultimately, goes hand in hand with innovation. Too often though, these types of authentic and personal learning experiences are the exception, not the norm. When done consistently over time, a long-lasting legacy is built. Being an educator is the greatest profession in the world, as you get to leave your fingerprints of impact on the lives you serve for generations to come. There's no doubt you'll be remembered, but it's *how you'll be remembered* that ultimately matters most. It won't be about *your* content; it'll be about *their experiences.*

How will you unleash the amazing potential that walks through your doors each day? What will their most empowering learning experiences look like? What will your legacy ultimately be?

I have no doubt that, like me, you'll absolutely love this book.

Throughout the thoughtful words and meaningful ideas written on these pages, Cooper and Murphy, two renowned thought leaders in project based learning and inquiry-based learning, will navigate you through some of the most challenging aspects of PBL, while leaving you inspired by their stories and empowered with practical examples. Simultaneously, by confronting the status quo, Cooper and Murphy will motivate you to reflect on your own practices, while supporting you in creating the project based learning experiences today's modern learners need to succeed in life. And, you'll also be building your dynamic legacy along the way.

Are you ready? Let's go!

All for the kids we serve,

Thomas C. Murray
Director of Innovation, Future Ready Schools
Author of *Personal & Authentic: Designing Learning Experiences That Impact a Lifetime*
@thomascmurray

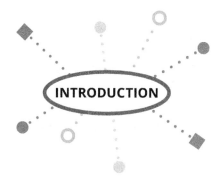

Why Project Based Learning?

Ask the right questions, and the answers
will always reveal themselves.
— OPRAH WINFREY, TALK SHOW HOST

ROSS'S WHY

IN 1990, I completed first grade at New Haven Hebrew Day School in Orange, Connecticut. Because my mother held onto all of my old report cards and more, I can tell you that my teacher, Mrs. Winters, wrote the following comments on my report card for the fourth and final marking period:

> Ross has made very good academic growth in English this year. He enjoys learning when it's something he's interested in. He still has difficulty complying to rules if his interest lies somewhere else. Have a happy and healthy summer. Fondly, Mary Winters

Mrs. Winters's sentiments were more or less an ongoing theme throughout my time as a student, and also sometimes during my time as an adult. Although I was crazy about learning, I never exactly loved school; too much time was spent on things that simply didn't interest me. As a result, I often misbehaved.

An anonymous quote declares, "Be who you needed when you were younger." This is my why for becoming an educator, and this is my why for project based learning. I adore students, and I'll endlessly promote learning experiences such as project based learning that allow for students to take ownership of their education. As a student, I didn't have many of these types of opportunities; now I want to create them for others.

ERIN'S WHY

During my senior year of college, I participated in an internship program that focused on teaching through project based and inquiry-based learning. At the time, I recognized that this type of learning was different from my experience in school; however, the benefits were clear: The learners in my second grade classroom demonstrated a deep understanding of their learning, as evidenced by their conversations, written responses, and product creation. Over the course of the year, I came to know this type of learning as the norm. But when I graduated and got my first teaching position, I found that the project based approach was actually the exception in the majority of schools. I was baffled by the reliance on basal readers, textbooks, and worksheets; I couldn't understand why those resources were used when more engaging and effective methods existed.

Now, as the parent of two daughters, I have a different lens. My girls are incredibly curious and have an insatiable thirst for learning. They describe "discovering something new" as their favorite hobby. I worry about education systems that might make my daughters, or any child, feel that learning is just about moving information from a textbook to a worksheet rather than the thrill of discovery. My why boils down to my belief that children deserve to have learning experiences that inspire curiosity and foster joy.

OUR APPROACH

Whenever we involve ourselves in project based learning, we think back to why we first decided to embrace this approach. These reasons serve as motivation and help us humanize the work. After all, our curriculum work won't matter if what we do doesn't resonate with people on a personal level.

Meanwhile, we realize that not everyone is as passionate about project based learning as we are. Your passion might equal or exceed ours, or maybe you strongly dislike project based learning, but are doing it because you've been told you have to. Either way, because you're tackling project based learning in one way or another, let's take a look at how this approach can benefit both you and your students and why you may want to prioritize project based learning to shift the instruction in your classroom, school, or district.

PBL PROMOTES RELEVANCE (NOT JUST ENGAGEMENT)

Based on what we've experienced, countless schools prioritize what's comfortable for adults, not what's best for students. And then we take issue with students when they don't buy into what we're doing.

While these misplaced priorities can present themselves in many ways, shapes, and forms, one manifestation involves student voice and choice, or a lack thereof. According to the Quaglia Institute School Voice Report (2016), 56 percent of students feel like they don't have a voice in decision-making at school, and partially as a result, 43 percent of students think school is boring. While many of us may believe we're giving our students voice and choice, it's easy to fall into the trap of convincing ourselves of that when it's just not true.

Ross: As a fourth grade teacher and foodie, I often gave my students a Top Chef project, which required them to write restaurant reviews. Each student went to a restaurant of their choice, took notes throughout the dining process, and then converted the notes to a professional-looking review that was posted on a blog and sent to the restaurant. Students who couldn't make it to a restaurant reviewed home cooking, which was always fun ... but also controversial.

When we tell educators about this project, they're typically hooked. But when we pick apart the project, we find that I never asked my students if *they* were foodies or if *they* were interested in writing about restaurants. Looking back, I could have presented Top Chef to students as one of several ways to demonstrate their learning, while also letting them come up with options of their own. Or, as a starting point, I could have asked students whether they wanted to write restaurant reviews.

Student voice and choice can be the difference between engagement (trying to get students excited about *our* interests) and relevance (providing opportunities for students to get excited about *their* interests). While selling students on our interests tends to generate engagement that is oftentimes short-lived, the latter approach starts with the students and prioritizes what makes them unique. As a result, they are the designers or co-designers of relevant learning experiences that tap into their intrinsic motivation.

When we consider students owning the learning, teacher and student comfort levels will vary based on context. For example, teachers may not be ready to give up control, and students may not know how to act when they have control. Regardless, we should always move toward student ownership in one way or another. But this transition is easier said than done, and many of us may be left wondering how to make it happen.

In this regard, project based learning is instrumental because it gives us a solid but flexible framework that lends itself to student voice, choice, and relevance. If these elements aren't involved, we believe what we're doing isn't project based learning. There are two main reasons why project based learning goes hand in hand with voice, choice, and relevance.

One, because project based learning has us planning for the long term, we have less urgency for students to demonstrate *this learning, this way, right now*. We have flexibility in terms of how and when because instead we are looking for students to meet their goals in some way, shape, or form by the end of the project, and even then, we can give extensions. Simon Sinek beautifully and succinctly summed up these circumstances when he said, "When we have a clear sense of where we're going, we are flexible in how we get there."

Two, every PBL unit generally involves at least one project in which students create a product, contribute to an event, or tackle a problem. In much the same way students (and adults) read with bias, and therefore can never truly read within "the four corners of the text," students will never be able to work within "the four corners of a project." Unless we're giving them step-by-step directions (which we shouldn't), students will attack their projects in ways that are unique to who they are, based on their strengths, experiences, and background knowledge.

Students who aren't accustomed to project based learning will, at times, seek permission and/or support to take advantage of all of this flexibility and autonomy. Students who are comfortable with project based learning, though, throw themselves into their work as if it's their right to do so—and it is.

Relevancy isn't something we do *to* students. Rather, we create the conditions for students to take ownership of their work. Project based learning can help to make these conditions a reality.

PBL HELPS US WORK SMARTER, NOT HARDER

Most of us probably remember the traditional lesson plans we had to hand in as pre-service teachers. Many of them followed the Madeline Hunter lesson plan model: lesson objectives, standards addressed, anticipatory set, teaching/instructional process, guided practice and monitoring, closure, independent practice. All of our unit plans may also have consisted of several lesson plans in unnecessarily large three-ring binders, connected by nothing more than an overarching topic.

We believe these types of units are still prevalent in many of our schools. Here's an idea of what it typically looks like in action:

1. Teacher introduces a topic, such as the three branches of government.

2. Students are exposed to said topic through a series of lessons, which may or may not be distributed as a packet. As students learn, formative assessments help guide instruction.

3. Students are tested on the information they learned from the lessons.

4. Everyone moves on to the next unit.

While there are several problems with this approach, here are three to consider. 1) The entire unit, or the majority of it, is laid out without thinking about the students on its receiving end (an eerily similar unit may even be taught again next year). 2) Unless students are in love with the three branches of government, there's no incentive for them to learn the material other than to do well on a test. 3) It is never clarified for students what they should *know*, *understand*, and *be able to do* as a result of studying the three branches of government. Therefore, the unit lacks true direction and feels as if the teacher is trying to cram a complex topic into inadequate instructional time by feeding students facts that they are then required to regurgitate.

This lesson-by-lesson approach is flawed because we're planning to teach in a way that doesn't maximize student learning. In other words, we're working way too hard to execute something that doesn't actually work. Project based learning can help us work smarter, not harder. As a holistic approach to instructional planning, project based learning is, at its core, an inquiry-based instructional unit—a unit in which students learn primarily through investigation and exploration.

During project based learning, we provide valuable context when students continuously apply what they learn to at least one project while ideally meeting its learning goals. These goals align with what we want students to know, understand, and be able to do, and the goals are usually assessed with a rubric or something similar. The push and pull between parts (individual lessons) and whole (project) is crucial, as projects serve as the glue that bonds individual lessons with the overall learning experience. Students develop a deeper understanding of content as they engage in productive struggle when applying their learning to a project. In the absence of a project, teaching and learning has nothing to latch onto, so it possesses far less substance. This is equivalent to learning a whole bunch of discrete facts and skills and then never having an opportunity to apply the information.

While the shift to project based learning may sound intimidating, it can be a win-win. Students get to learn *through* project based learning and inquiry, while teachers aren't forced to embrace the daily grind of figuring out what they want to teach and how to teach it. Additionally, we're able to tackle several academic standards at the same time in an authentic context, as opposed to lesson plans that typically address one or two standards at a time in isolation.

As teachers, we facilitated project based learning experiences that were as short as two weeks and as long as about ten weeks. Some of these did take quite some time to plan. However, with each unit, our planning became more efficient. And while a considerable amount of planning should be done prior to the launch of a project based learning experience, that planning means there's less for you to proactively plan day to day. Instead of asking ourselves what we're going to teach and how, we can spend more time responding to students' needs throughout the learning process. Yes, this work can still be tiring, but it helps us meet students where they are. Meanwhile, we get to avoid the burnout that can come from daily planning.

Taking a holistic approach to teaching also helps promote ongoing collaboration among educators. Special education teachers regularly work with classroom teachers to support students with Individualized Education Programs (IEPs). Toward the beginning of our careers, we gave the special education teachers an outline of our plans for the following week every Friday, and they adapted it.

This process wasn't ideal, as it gave us "one more thing" to do every Friday, and lessons had to be adapted at the last minute. Fast forward a few years into our teaching careers when we shifted to project based learning. As a result, rather than sharing weekly plans, we formally met with the special education teachers every three to four weeks and discussed what was coming, giving them more than enough time to adapt the units for students with IEPs, if necessary. Just as importantly, we developed shared ownership of our classrooms, as we were all operating with a long-term vision.

PBL PROVIDES CONTEXT FOR PROFESSIONAL LEARNING

Here's an ironic scenario: Like many administrators and teacher leaders, early in our careers, we may have been overwhelmed by the number of initiatives we had to endure, and we may have even gone around badmouthing our administrators. We promised ourselves we would never do to others what had been done to us. Then, when we finally had a say in professional learning, those on the receiving end also claimed they were overwhelmed.

As administrators, we have opportunities to take the lead in facilitating instructional shifts and professional learning. And, both of us have had teachers voice their concerns to us about being overwhelmed, even though we had promised ourselves this would never be the case. What we have learned is that friction is a part of any change process, and no matter how intentional we are, there will still be those who criticize in one way or another. Nonetheless, as we interact with these educators, we can still 1) seek to understand where they're coming from while asking ourselves what we can do differently, and 2) ascertain whether their voices represent the majority.

Even so, the fact remains that initiative fatigue is a reality in countless schools and districts, maybe even our own. It is easy for administrators to lose track of everything teachers have to do on a daily, weekly, and monthly basis.

Doug Reeves (2010) reiterates this sentiment while also pointing us in the right direction:

> The clear imperative for educational leadership is focus. Unfortunately, the typical response of leaders at every

23

level is diffusion, often in the guise of strategic plans. ... Large-scale improvement is most likely to occur when a few school initiatives are implemented deeply, not when a laundry list of initiatives is implemented in a scatter-shot manner.

Project based learning can help to give us this focus.

In *Hacking Project Based Learning* (2016), we revealed, "The more we have familiarized ourselves with project based learning, the more we have come to realize it is a series of best practices joined together." These practices, many of which can be used with or without project based learning, include but are not limited to: establishing a culture of inquiry and creativity, designing flexible learning spaces, teaching collaboration skills, facilitating student self-assessment, elevating student learning with conferencing and feedback, integrating direction instruction, using formative assessments to drive instruction, student publishing, and student reflection.

OUR WORDS AND ACTIONS MUST COMMUNICATE THAT THE THOUGHTS AND IDEAS OF OTHERS CAN MAKE A DIFFERENCE.

Looking at these practices, many of them are probably synonymous with the instructional shifts or professional learning sessions that have transpired in our schools and districts. When presented in isolation, they read and feel like Reeves's overwhelming "laundry list of initiatives." When presented within the context of project based learning, we're not as overwhelmed, and we (and our students) are much more capable of seeing and feeling how all of these pieces fit together to enhance teaching and learning.

Additionally, by viewing project based learning as a series of best practices, as opposed to a framework that must be tackled all at once (either you're doing it or you're not), our transition to project based learning can exist along a continuum with multiple entry points. For example, too often a group of teachers is told something like, "Everyone must engage their students in at least one project based learning experience." Depending on our current teaching style, this shift may be overwhelming. But, based on our students' strengths and needs, our comfort level, and available resources, we may be able to successfully implement certain components of project based learning, such as flexible learning spaces and student publishing. If this is the case, we should be applauded for our willingness to take risks and move forward, and we should continue to grow until what we're doing can be considered project based learning (and even then, there is room for improvement).

The challenge, then, is to focus on project based learning and not much else, as it takes a great deal of time for any new approach to stick on a systemic level. As Jim Collins (2001) wrote in *Good to Great*, we must "create a 'stop doing list' and systematically unplug anything extraneous." When planning professional learning, it's best to choose a distinct direction and stick with it while providing room for some teacher choice. We need to resist the urge to continuously schedule "learning detours" by jumping at the latest and greatest or whatever may appear to be urgent.

At the same time, teachers (and administrators) can be encouraged to take charge of their own learning instead of always waiting for "district direction" or a professional development day. In schools and districts with a healthy culture, just about anyone can initiate and lead change. In much the same way teachers empower students, administrators should be empowering teachers (and everyone else). Bottom line: *Our words and actions must communicate that the thoughts and ideas of others can make a difference.*

PBL MAKES US FUTURE READY

If we want to move forward, we need to know why, and we need to know how. We never lose sight of the why; it isn't something we touch on at the beginning of an instructional shift and then never return to again. And we can never be too explicit about the how; strategies and frameworks should be as clear as we can make them.

For both of us, our why is encompassed by the question: Are we meeting students where they are, or are we forcing them to conform to us?

For the purpose of this book, project based learning is the how, which, believe it or not, we sometimes only gloss over. According to the Organization for Economic Cooperation and Development (OECD) website, "Futures Thinking is a method for informed reflection on the major changes that will occur in the next ten, twenty, or more years in all areas of social life, including education." Daily, we bump into several "Futures" articles and resources as we scroll through our social media feeds, and we have heard countless educators and speakers call for schools to change with such lines as, "85 percent of our students' future jobs don't even exist yet!" We get it. And while we believe this kind of talk does have a place in PBL professional learning, waxing poetic about the future shouldn't supplant the hard work of following up with the how. Most of us simply want practical strategies to move our students forward.

Entire books have been written about how our schools are failing our kids, and how the world has changed but our education system, for the most part, has not. This is not one of those books. This book is about practicality, the how. But, we want to leave you with information to consider.

Every year, the National Association of Colleges and Employers conducts a survey to find out the attributes that employers look for in prospective employees. According to the most current report as of this writing, *Job Outlook 2020*, here are the top ten skills, in order:

1. Problem-solving skills

2. Ability to work in a team

3. Strong work ethic

4. Analytical/quantitative skills

5. Communication skills (written)

6. Leadership

7. Communication skills (verbal)

8. Initiative

9. Detail-oriented

10. Technical skills

An objective look at these skills can tell us whether or not our schools are developing these skills in our students.

Many schools and districts are moving forward by placing an emphasis on the 4 Cs: critical thinking, communication, collaboration, and creativity. While this is certainly a starting point, there should also be a common definition and understanding of what these terms entail. Plus, when we only address these skills in isolation, we send the message that they function independently, as opposed to being part of a process that leads to a deeper understanding of content and an enhanced skill set. We can attach these skills to the process of project based learning.

Countless other surveys and studies have called for changes to the education system. One such study, published in 2015 by McKinsey & Company, concludes:

The bottom line is that 45 percent of work activities could be automated using already demonstrated technology. If the technologies that process and "understand" natural language were to reach the median level of human performance, an additional 13 percent of work activities in the US economy could be automated.

Considering current technologies, facts are ubiquitous. Facts are free. And if the majority of our teaching focuses on facts or work students can accomplish entirely on their own, we should ask ourselves why we're doing what we're doing.

Regarding student engagement at school, Gallup has surveyed more than five million students from grades five through twelve. Overall, 29 percent of students claim to be "not engaged," and 24 percent of students claim to be "actively disengaged." In general, there is a slow and steady decline in engagement as students progress through school. Across all grade levels, only 30 percent of teachers report high levels of engagement. These results are followed by action steps, which conclude: "Building a culture of engagement is not an event; it's a process that requires intentional and sustained effort. And while it is not always easy to create engagement, it is absolutely worth the investment" (Hodges, 2018).

Project based learning can help us build this culture and more.

REAL QUESTIONS

In December 2016, we published *Hacking Project Based Learning: 10 Easy Steps to PBL and Inquiry in the Classroom*, which demystifies what PBL is all about with ten hacks that educators and students can follow to achieve success.

Since the release of this book, we have had the privilege of meeting and working with thousands of educators who are making project based learning a reality in their classrooms. Countless additional educators from across the globe would love to leverage project based learning to create learner-centered opportunities for their students.

Nonetheless, based on our experiences, we know that project based learning has yet to go mainstream. If so many educators believe in project based learning, and if project based learning can benefit so many of our students, why isn't this approach the norm?

Because educators have questions.

Prior to each workshop or speaking engagement, some of which are facilitated in our own districts, we spend time preparing our talking points, slide decks, and learning activities. But our favorite part of collaborating with educators is the conversations that happen off-script. The questions posed by participants demonstrate the cognitive work of connecting new information to existing knowledge, and they allow us to connect with each person as a learner while providing the information they need most.

After a while, patterns emerged in the most common questions, and we began to anticipate what teachers would ask us. As any good educator would do, we started to proactively incorporate these questions and our answers into our presentations. However, we felt we could do more to share this work with a larger audience.

We wrote this book because educators have questions, and we wanted to share our responses on a larger scale to make them accessible to everyone who wants to improve teaching and learning.

REAL ANSWERS

Before we go any further, it is important that we address the word "real" from our title. "Real" is not synonymous with "right," and this is an important distinction. Few questions in education have precisely one right answer, and instructional methods, like project based learning, are no exception.

By real, we mean honest.

We aren't selling a program or a prescription. Our answers are based on our often hard-earned experiences and approachable solutions, which we have practiced and recommended to educators with whom we work. We often refer to project based learning implementation as a continuum, and as such, it comes with multiple entry points. Our goal, always, is to offer practitioners what they need to feel successful in their work regardless of where they begin.

USING THIS BOOK

While this book answers questions and dives into the thick of project based learning, an ongoing theme is the idea that project based learning isn't presented in isolation or as the silver bullet for meeting our students' needs. In this sense, this book reads more like a progressive educator toolkit that can serve as a resource for those who want or need to make their practices more relevant, while adding value for those already moving forward.

Because project based learning is a conglomerate of tried-and-true practices, you'll be able to find a significant amount of research regarding any single element. When appropriate, we include a sampling of this research within our answers. We stand on the shoulders of giants, and we respect the work of other authors and practitioners. Other times, we intentionally reference certain pieces of work (e.g., books, videos, TED Talks), making it easier for you to extend your learning, if you choose. All resources are available on the book's website: realpbl.com. Our Facebook group, which includes thousands of like-minded members, can be found at facebook.com/groups/realpbl.

During a presentation, common questions from participants

always emerge in a different order. The same is true for this book. You do not need to read the chapters in a specific order. Choose a chapter that works for you as a starting point, and go from there. If you choose to read this book front to back, your questions will be answered and you will, in the process, take the steps toward learning how to do project based learning. In other words, all of our answers strung together detail project based learning in its entirety, pieced together through the chapters.

FINAL THOUGHTS

As avid readers, we're constantly on the lookout for books we can recommend to other educators, as putting the right books in the hands of our colleagues can help propel transformative learning experiences for our students. Consequently, we're always reading, and we know the most powerful education books aren't just the books that shift our thinking, but those that shift our thinking and our actions. We believe *Project Based Learning* is one of these books.

Finally, because we need to be lifelong learners, and because we need to model what this looks like for our students and colleagues, we've never stopped overthinking what we included in our first book. Although you won't find glaring discrepancies between the two, the book you're holding in your hands represents our current, best, and most complete thinking on project based learning. And, no matter where your current thinking may be, we are confident our words and ideas will inspire you along your journey.

Let's get started.

For chapter resources, visit realpbl.com/resources. Join the discussion online using the hashtag #RealPBL.

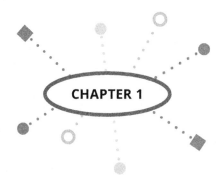

CHAPTER 1

REAL QUESTION:

How Do I Structure a PBL Experience?

A list of content and activities is not a plan.
— GRANT WIGGINS AND JAY MCTIGHE, AUTHORS OF *SCHOOLING BY DESIGN*

NOT LONG AGO, we facilitated three days of PBL professional learning for a group of about forty educators. Following a brief introduction, we asked everyone in the room, including administrators, to take about five minutes to write down their definition of project based learning. Once their definitions were recorded, participants shared their work in small groups, and then everyone in the room came together to share. As participants spoke, we completed a T-Chart: the left side was titled "Differences," and the right side was titled "Commonalities."

Afterward, we transitioned to discussing what we could conclude from the T-Chart and the activity as a whole. We realized that there was no shared definition of project based learning. This conclusion rang true for all educators in the room.

This type of confusion can certainly create a potential road-block, because for project based learning or any other instructional shift to happen, the larger group needs a common definition. This definition helps promote common language, collaboration, and a clear vision among those in-district. At the same time, an expanded definition containing the components of project based learning can serve as the floor or minimum expectation for what's expected in classrooms, while allowing teachers to exercise their creativity to make it their own.

Toward the end of the third day of professional learning, we worked together as a group to construct the district's definition of project based learning. They gained ownership of their definition, as they developed it in-house as part of a learning process, as opposed to being copied and pasted from somewhere else. And yes, there's nothing wrong with one district's definition being slightly different than another's.

Now, rewind to about ten years ago. We were both working for the East Penn School District in Macungie, Pennsylvania, when we first began facilitating PBL professional learning with our session "Project-Based Learning—Yes, I Can!" During our early years of facilitating project based learning, we presented under the assumption that our participants had no knowledge of the topic. As a result, we talked about project based learning as if it were an entirely unique entity, and we helped participants design projects from the ground up, with zero reliance on their previous work.

However, what we soon uncovered was that most educators were already doing projects but were not necessarily doing project based learning. In retrospect, this shouldn't have been so surprising, but since then, we have generally approached professional learning as if we're collaborating with participants to transition from projects to project based learning, as opposed to building something from nothing. This approach is beneficial for two reasons. First, we're not throwing out past work. With so many instructional shifts, the message often comes out as, "Forget everything you were doing. That was wrong. This is right." This approach disrespects the work that came before us and promotes initiative fatigue. Second, we're making the work easier because we're meeting educators where they are and helping them build on top of something they've already been doing. It's often (but not always) easier to create something from something, rather than something from nothing.

Let's take a look at the differences between projects and project based learning. As you read, we encourage you to formulate two definitions of project based learning: a one-sentence version, and an expanded version that can serve as the floor for what you expect of yourself in your classroom (teacher) or what's expected across classrooms (administrator).

Disclaimer 1 of 2: Throughout the book, for simplicity, we refer to project based learning experiences as "projects." There are exceptions in this chapter, when the term "projects" is used to reference old-school projects in order to contrast them with project based learning.

REAL ANSWERS:

IDENTIFY OLD-SCHOOL PROJECTS

For the most part, these are the types of projects we all completed when we were students. Based on our experiences, they still exist in the majority of classrooms. These projects can serve as a starting point for project based learning. Anyone who's adept at project based learning, including us, got their foot in the door by first implementing existing projects and then steadily improving upon their craft over time, until what they were doing could be considered project based learning. This transition doesn't happen overnight, but rather through an ongoing, gradual process of reflection and refinement. So, in short, projects aren't the problem; the problem is viewing those projects as the endgame rather than an entry point into something greater.

The majority of projects follow a predictable, linear process that has been laid out by the teacher without much, if any, student input. Here's a narrative of what the planning process can look like from the teacher's point of view.

> In two weeks, I know I have to teach [insert topic], and I'd like to jazz things up a bit! So, I'll teach just like I've done in the past, but then students will work in small groups to create [insert product]. All of this will probably take a couple of weeks. And to keep things a surprise, I won't tell students about the project until all of the teaching is finished, but I'll let them know before the topic's culminating test. This way, they can apply what they've learned from the project on the test!
>
> To make sure my students follow directions and get a good grade, I'll grade them on their ability to follow directions. My rubric will look just like my directions, but instead of being written in paragraphs, it'll be written as a list. For each item on the list, I'll include how much I think it should be worth. In all, there will probably be about thirty points. I'll determine students' grades by simply dividing their final score by thirty, or whatever ends up being the total number of possible points.
>
> As students are working, I'll walk around and help them with the directions. And, if several students struggle with a specific part, I'll form a group to show them what

to do. Finally, because we need to take the test and move on to the next topic, all work will be due by [insert date].

This narrative, or a similar one, has probably gone through all of our heads at one time or another. Consider the following questions and commentary as they relate to each of the three paragraphs.

Paragraph 1

- Why do all students have to create the exact same teacher-determined product?

- Why wait until after the teaching to tell students about the project? If we tell them ahead of time, they'll get excited, and all content will be more relevant, as they'll learn it within the context of the project.

- If students are able to demonstrate their learning through the project, why have them demonstrate their learning again by taking a test?

Paragraph 2

- If we're grading students on their ability to follow directions, aren't we grading compliance?

- Shouldn't we be grading students on their ability to meet our academic standards?

- Is it a defensible practice to convert a raw score (e.g., twenty-five out of thirty) into a percentage grade?

Paragraph 3

- As students are working, if all we're doing is helping them with directions, when does the actual learning take place during the project?

- Can we put systems in place for students to confidently help each other and possibly themselves? That way, students wouldn't have to always turn to us for help or approval.

- Is a firm due date entirely necessary?

Questions such as these, and an in-depth analysis of a project, can transition you from doing a project to doing project based learning without you even knowing it.

Old-school projects generally start with a topic, and then project time is spent on activities that relate to the topic in one way or another. This approach usually promotes surface-level learning, equivalent to students memorizing a list of facts while engaged in work that is hands-on, not necessarily minds-on.

DEFINE PROJECT BASED LEARNING

The alternative to old-school projects is project based learning, in which students uncover deeper understandings of content *while* they are working through a project. Ideally, by the time the project is complete, students will have had multiple opportunities to demonstrate this knowledge. While traditional instruction often paints a black-and-white picture of student acquisition of content—they get it or they don't—PBL allows for students to demonstrate understanding and go deeper than just "getting it." So, what exactly leads to a deeper understanding? Start by taking into account two main factors: productive struggle and context.

Productive struggle. Students are learning about electrical circuits. Rather than memorizing definitions and being told exactly how to build circuits, they're given wires, batteries, and light bulbs. They're asked to find all the ways they can make their bulbs light up. Afterward, they reflect on what they noticed. The definitions of simple circuit, parallel circuit, conductor, and insulator are only provided after the majority of students have a conceptual understanding of what circuits involve.

Context. This activity becomes more relevant and useful when presented within the context of a project based learning experience, such as students engineering their own pinball machines. Students can then use their knowledge of electrical circuits during the creation of their machines to gain a deeper understanding of how machines function.

Project based learning is both inspiring and scary. When we first took the dive into project based learning, we immersed ourselves in countless books, articles, and videos, many of which are still popular today. While what we experienced was inspiring because it's what we wanted our classrooms to be, it was scary because we didn't exactly know how to get there. In working with educators from across the country, we have found the majority of them feel the same way.

Project based learning is an inquiry-based instructional unit in which students learn primarily through investigation and exploration. To truly conceptualize what project based learning involves, our first step is to familiarize ourselves with the planning process. For this, we leverage backward design, or "beginning with the end in mind," which calls for us to begin our planning by considering what we want to be our students' main takeaways from the learning. More specifically, we can break this process into three steps: plan with the end in mind, plan the assessments, and plan the teaching and learning. If you reread the project narrative from earlier in this chapter, you'll see that the three paragraphs loosely follow these three steps—steps that we adapted from *Understanding by Design* (Wiggins and McTighe, 2005).

Let's take a look at what goes into the planning of a project based learning experience. We'll break down the process one step at a time, part by part, and then conclude with a revision of the project narrative. Although everything is presented in a linear fashion, it will, of course, be necessary to jump around as part of the ongoing revision process. An editable version of our project planning template and four sample projects in the template can be found at realpbl.com.

✗ STEP 1: PLAN WITH THE END IN MIND

When planning a PBL unit, there are five potential starting points, none of which are mutually exclusive.

- **Students:** Find out what's relevant to the students and use this as the basis for the project.

- **Cool idea:** Start with a cool idea that gets your students and/or you excited.

- **A process:** Build your project around a process, such as design thinking or the engineering cycle.

- **The end in mind:** Establish what you want your students' main takeaways (what we refer to as High Impact Takeaways) to be, and plan backward from there.

- **Academic standards:** Flip through your academic standards, looking for inspiration, which can come from standards that promote learning that is hands-on, minds-on, and interdisciplinary.

No matter where we begin, our project should connect to the standards, unless students are engaged in something like Genius Hour (detailed in Chapter 8), or our organization isn't held accountable for the standards.

While formulating ideas, you can also rely on the three tracks of project based learning, which range from most restrictive to least restrictive. Think of these tracks as a gradual release of responsibility, starting with Product Track and ending with Open-Ended Track.

- **Product Track:** All students create a product(s) or contribute to an event, but there's flexibility regarding how they do it so students can exercise their creativity to own the process.

- **Problem Track:** The project starts with a problem (usually a real-world problem) that either the teacher gives to students or students find on their own. This approach is often referred to as problem-based learning or challenge-based learning.

- **Open-Ended Track:** Present students with the project's High Impact Takeaways, learning targets, and possibly an Umbrella Question, and ask them to demonstrate their knowledge however they'd like, with only a little more direction.

One track isn't necessarily better than another. For any given project, choose the track that fits best with your specific context. For example, even when you and/or your students are comfortable with the Open-Ended Track, it might be more appropriate to use the Product Track, depending on what you want to accomplish. And yes, you might use more than one track during a PBL unit—students debating an issue (Product Track) in the midst of solving a problem (Problem Track)—but one track tends to drive the unit as a whole.

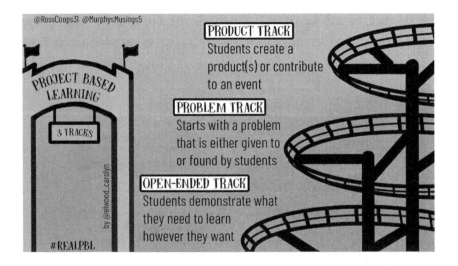

Project title

If the title connects to something that already exists (movie, band, video game), amplify your project's materials with ready-made graphics and fonts.

Here are five generic titles, each followed by an alternative to which students might better relate.

- Movie Trailers; replace with Coming Attractions (an authentic spin).

- The Pinball Project; replace with Pinball Wizard (from *Tommy*).

- Solar-Powered Cars; replace with Need for Speed: Solar Rollers (like the video game).

- Farm to Table; replace with Green Cuisine (instead of Lean Cuisine).

- Endangered Animals; replace with Angry Animals (instead of Angry Birds).

High Impact Content and Supporting Content

High Impact Content are the select few academic standards that serve as the basis for the project. These standards typically call for a deeper understanding of content (e.g., apply, understand, explain). Supporting Content refers to the ancillary standards that call for more surface-level learning (e.g., define, recognize, identify). In the context of project based learning, these standards support the High Impact Content. To promote interdisciplinary learning, use standards (High Impact Content and/or Supporting Content) from across multiple subject areas. Although students likely will touch upon multiple standards throughout a project, a good rule of thumb is to plan with about eight total standards in mind—a number that can vary, mostly based on project length. These are the standards that will be formally assessed and possibly graded. As we select and read through these standards, we should be able to visualize how students might tackle them as they work through their projects.

Why is this component needed and who is it for?

Connecting your project to the standards means you make the project the learning, as opposed to a fun activity after the "real learning" is finished. State testing assesses students on their knowledge of those standards, and connecting them to your project helps debunk the myth that project based learning can't prepare students for those tests.

High Impact Content and Supporting Content are for the teacher or for whoever is planning the project. When we put standards in the hands of students, we do so in the form of learning targets, which are student-friendly standards.

High Impact Takeaways (also called enduring understandings)

These are our students' main takeaways from the project, or in other words, the morals of the project. When generating High

Impact Takeaways, make sure all your High Impact Content is accounted for in one way or another. For instance, you may create one High Impact Takeaway for each piece of High Impact Content, or create one or two High Impact Takeaways that encompass all High Impact Content.

Additionally, consider these questions when crafting your High Impact Takeaways:

- Do the High Impact Takeaways promote inquiry as opposed to rote memorization?

- Are the High Impact Takeaways in student-friendly language? Do they promote student ownership?

Why is this component needed and who is it for?

You end up with surface-level learning when you try to cover an entire topic with a project. By planning with High Impact Takeaways in mind, you're asking yourself what your students' main takeaways should be, or what you want them to remember when they graduate. This approach helps focus your project planning and teaching, and as a result, helps you present the project in a way that allows students to learn on a deeper level.

When you put High Impact Takeaways in student-friendly language, you have the option of making them available to students. They may still contain academic language, though, so giving them to students too early can lead to confusion, while also potentially spoiling what students are supposed to get out of the project. When you're thinking about communicating the High Impact Takeaways to students, ask yourself *when* you should make it happen.

While it is challenging to gauge the effectiveness of a High Impact Takeaway without the context of an entire project, here are five examples:

- Reading helps us learn new information and make decisions.

- Writing can make meaning of one's own experiences.

- Shapes in design and construction can create safe, supportive structures.

- Patterns and relationships can be represented numerically, graphically, symbolically, and verbally.

- Water can be purified to create a potable liquid.

Umbrella Question (also called essential questions)

The Umbrella Question is all of the High Impact Takeaways wrapped into one question, and it serves as the project's branding. You should be able to draw a straight line from the High Impact Content and Supporting Content (academic standards) to the High Impact Takeaways and finally to the Umbrella Question. Figure 1.2 illustrates this straight line with Take Action, a project in which students pursue the civic processes necessary to solve a local problem while comparing their rights to the rights of citizens in historic contexts.

As the Umbrella Question is the project's branding, consider including it toward the top of all project-related materials so students can see how it relates to everything they're learning. As teachers, we posted our current unit's Umbrella Question in the front of the room for everyone to see at all times. If we were to create a mind map of all project-related content, the Umbrella Question would sit right in the center as the project's main idea or as the glue that holds everything together.

During and at the conclusion of the project, have students make explicit connections between the learning and the Umbrella Question. For example, after a project-related activity, ask them to write or blog about what they've learned and how it relates to the Umbrella Question. In time, as students become familiar with what an Umbrella Question involves, ask them to contribute to or create as a class each project's Umbrella Question. As students take their project in different directions, each individual or group can design their own "Mini Umbrella Question" for their specific work. We call these guiding questions.

Additionally, consider these three questions when crafting your Umbrella Question:

- Does the Umbrella Question promote inquiry as opposed to rote memorization? During a project, it should feel as if students are interrogating the Umbrella Question.

- Will the Umbrella Question elicit multiple responses as opposed to one definitive answer? In other words, is it Googleable?

- Has the Umbrella Question been written in a way that is short, compact, and conversational, almost as if it could be repeated like a mantra?

For reference, here are five Umbrella Questions. Once again, without the context of an entire project, it is challenging to gauge their effectiveness:

- How does where you live affect how you live?

- How important is a constitution?

- What if you want to change a law?

- In adversity, why do some prevail while others fail?

- How can patterns help me become a more efficient problem-solver?

Figure 1.1 illustrates how we can derive a project's Umbrella Question from a project's High Impact Takeaway.

HIGH IMPACT TAKEAWAYS	UMBRELLA QUESTIONS
Claims and counterclaims use evidence and organization to be effective.	What is an effective argument?
We read to learn new information and make decisions.	Why do we read?
Properties of operations can be used to multiply and divide numbers.	Which properties matter the most?
Fossils document the history of life forms.	How does a fossil tell its story?
Our government has powers, responsibilities, and limits that change and are contested.	Who has power?

FIGURE 1.1 - Turning High Impact Takeaways Into Umbrella Questions

High Impact Takeaways and Umbrella Questions transcend context in that they reference the learning, not the specifics of their project. This kind of language can help students apply their learning to unique situations and contexts beyond the project itself. This is called transfer of learning. One Umbrella Question subcategory worth mentioning is the driving question—what an Umbrella Question is sometimes referred to when it's more project-specific (e.g., "How might we redesign our classroom?"). Other than this one difference, a driving question should be crafted and used in much the same way as an Umbrella Question. We don't recommend worrying too much about the difference between these two types of questions, as oftentimes the line between them is blurred. Either way, ensure High Impact Takeaways always transcend context.

Finally, throughout the book, we discuss Umbrella Questions

as if each project should have only one. Ideally, for simplicity, this is what we want. But we also know there are instances, such as in Figure 1.2, in which a few Umbrella Questions are necessary to encompass students' learning.

Learning targets

These are the academic standards (High Impact Content and Supporting Content) in student-friendly language. Here are three tips to consider when converting standards to learning targets:

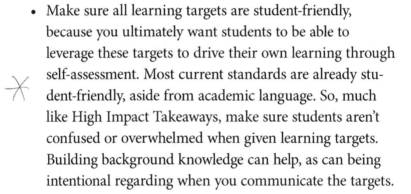

- If a standard contains multiple independent actions (e.g., I can identify a dog and a cat), split it up into multiple learning targets (e.g., I can identify a dog. I can identify a cat.).

- Make sure all learning targets are student-friendly, because you ultimately want students to be able to leverage these targets to drive their own learning through self-assessment. Most current standards are already student-friendly, aside from academic language. So, much like High Impact Takeaways, make sure students aren't confused or overwhelmed when given learning targets. Building background knowledge can help, as can being intentional regarding when you communicate the targets.

- To promote inquiry, present each learning target in the form of a question ("Can I ...?" instead of "I can ...").

Unlike standards, a project's learning targets should be made available to students. Learning targets should serve as the basis for a project's assessment (Step 2) and instruction (Step 3).

Step 1 is the most complex of the three steps. But if you take your time and are thoughtful about your decisions, the rest of the planning process becomes easier. Figure 1.2 illustrates Step 1 in its entirety.

PROJECT · GRADE · SUBJECT	Take Action / High School World Studies

PROJECT DESCRIPTION

Students learn about important historic leaders while examining how different leadership styles can impact the engagement of citizens. Students explore their personal civic rights and the associated civil processes, and compare their rights to the rights of individuals in the past as they attempt to solve a local problem. Historic examples for this project reach as far back as 200 AD. The student product is relevant to the civic process pursued.

HIGH IMPACT CONTENT & SUPPORTING CONTENT	HIGH IMPACT TAKEAWAYS	UMBRELLA QUESTION
High Impact Content D2.Civ.2.9-12.: Analyze the role of citizens in the U.S. political system, with attention to various theories of democracy, changes in Americans' participation over time, and alternative models from other countries, past and present. D2.Civ.8.9-12.: Evaluate social and political systems in different contexts, times, and places, that promote civic virtues and enact democratic principles. D2.His.4.9-12.: Analyze complex and interacting factors that influenced the perspectives of people during different historical eras. **Supporting Content** D1.1.9-12.: Individually and with other students construct compelling questions and explain how a question reflects an enduring issue in the field. D1.2.9-12.: Explain points of agreement and disagreement experts have about interpretations and applications of disciplinary concepts and ideas associated with a compelling question. D1.5.9-12.: Determine the kinds of sources that will be helpful in answering compelling and supporting questions, taking into consideration multiple points of view represented in the sources, the types of sources available, and the potential uses of the sources.	Citizens pursue civic action to make change. The rights of citizens are reliant upon historical and social contexts.	How can I pursue civic action to make change? How does civic action now compare to civic action of the past?

LEARNING TARGETS

I can analyze the role of citizens in the U.S. political system.
I can evaluate social and political systems in different contexts, times, and places.
I can analyze complex and interacting factors that influenced the perspectives of people during different historical eras.
I can construct a compelling question.
I can explain varying perspectives regarding a compelling question.
I can determine the kinds of sources that will be helpful in answering compelling questions.

FIGURE 1.2 - Project Planning Step 1

STEP 2: PLAN THE ASSESSMENTS

While Chapter 2 is dedicated to assessment and grading, here we'll stick to describing the Progress Assessment Tool, our simplified version of a rubric, to demonstrate the intentionality with which assessment (Step 2) connects to desired results (Step 1).

Most projects come with rubrics that are full of 4s, 3s, 2s, and 1s, and these numbers and all of their descriptors easily make our heads spin. If rubrics can do this to us, imagine the negative impact they can have on our students! Ultimately, you don't want a complex tool that holds your students accountable, but rather a simple tool that helps them drive their own learning through self-assessment and peer assessment.

We designed the Progress Assessment Tool, which is a three-column "rubric" that we give to students toward the start of a project. Here's what's in the three columns.

Left column: The project's learning targets. You're assessing students on what you want them to learn. You're not assessing them based on how well they follow the project's directions, a practice that promotes compliance. In other words, if your assessment tool looks like project directions regurgitated in another format, you need to redo it.

Middle column: Each learning target's success criteria. If you want students to have flexibility regarding how they demonstrate their learning, success criteria should be medium agnostic. Refrain from mentioning specific products, technologies, or tasks. The litmus test is to ask, "If teachers from other classrooms are teaching the same learning target in a different way, would they be able to use the same success criteria?" Optionally, students can work with the teacher to construct success criteria, as opposed to the teacher simply giving it to them. When possible, we accomplished this through the analysis of exemplars (e.g., students analyzing various narrative essay introductions in order to determine their quality features).

Here are five learning targets along with their success criteria:

- **Learning Target 1:** I can identify who is telling the story at various points in a text.

  Success Criteria 1: The response shares who is telling the story and mentions when the narrator changes.

- **Learning Target 2:** I can compare two fractions with different numerators and different denominators.

  Success Criteria 2: Two unlike fractions are compared. The response shows which is larger or smaller, or if they're equal.

- **Learning Target 3:** I can apply knowledge of basic electrical circuits to the design and construction of simple direct current circuits.

  Success Criteria 3: A closed circuit is designed and constructed. Elements can be added or subtracted while maintaining a closed circuit.

- **Learning Target 4:** I can construct arguments using precise and knowledgeable claims.

  Success Criteria 4: Source information is used to construct a clear claim. The claim is presented using domain-specific vocabulary.

- **Learning Target 5:** I can use analyzed data to determine whether a chemical reaction has occurred.

  Success Criteria 5: Based on the data analysis, specific patterns are presented. Data is used to make a decision about a scientific phenomenon.

LEARNING TARGETS	SUCCESS CRITERIA	FEEDBACK
I can analyze the role of citizens in the U.S. political system.	The explanation or interpretation demonstrates a close examination and deep understanding of the rights of a citizen.	
I can evaluate social and political systems in different contexts, times, and places.	A distinction is made between various political systems and civil rights across historic contexts. An opinion is stated regarding the effectiveness of various political systems.	
I can analyze complex and interacting factors that influenced the perspectives of people during different historical eras.	Influential factors relevant to the historic context are identified. The impact of the factors on the perspectives of people are examined and explained.	
I can construct a compelling question.	The project identifies a relevant problem. The problem is reasonably approachable.	
I can explain varying perspectives regarding a compelling question.	Varying perspectives from multiple sources are presented and explained.	
I can determine the kinds of sources that will be helpful in answering compelling questions.	Primary and secondary sources are utilized to inform the work. As applicable, content is gathered from a variety of sources: databases, official websites, print, etc.	

FIGURE 1.3 - Progress Assessment Tool

For standards-based grading, think of the middle column as a score of 3 out of 4, or proficient, with all other scores/numbers omitted for simplicity's sake. If you're working with percentage grades or letter grades instead of standards-based grading, think of the middle column as an A. Still, we caution against trying to get an official grade out of the Progress Assessment Tool, though Chapter 2 details this process.

Right column: Where feedback is given in relation to each target. Ideally, much of this feedback is self-assessment and peer assessment, but, of course, teachers will help.

Figure 1.3 provides an example of a Progress Assessment Tool.

If possible, we strongly recommend creating and distributing a digital version of the Progress Assessment Tool, potentially through Google Docs or Google Classroom. Housing this resource on a server or in the cloud makes it available to everyone at all times. Because it's digital, the cells/boxes will conveniently expand as we type into them.

For individual projects, every student receives a copy. For group projects, think about what you're going to group assess versus individually assess. Sometimes, group projects will contain a combination of the two. Each group gets a Progress Assessment Tool and so does each individual. On the group copy, give feedback on the group learning targets. On the individual copy, give feedback on the individual learning targets. Meanwhile, if you're able to individually assess students on all targets, every student gets their own Progress Assessment Tool. If every target will be group-assessed, do one copy per group. Also, while we don't advocate for grading the project itself, if a grade is necessary, try to avoid group grades. In these instances, refrain from using a group Progress Assessment Tool.

Disclaimer 2 of 2: Throughout the book, we explain ways in

which you can use the Progress Assessment Tool in the classroom. In many cases, you can adapt these ideas to make them work with a more traditional rubric or a similar assessment tool.

STEP 3: PLAN THE TEACHING AND LEARNING

Chapter 4 is dedicated to direct instruction and lessons taught throughout the PBL experience, most of which are planned with the project's learning targets in mind. Here, we'll stick to reflection and publishing, which are also part of Step 3. Of course, the two aren't mutually exclusive, as students can reflect while publishing through blog posts, websites, videos, and social media.

Reflection

We've seen teachers haphazardly tack reflection onto the end of a project because they were told that it's an essential element of project based learning and therefore needs to happen. And yes, we've been guilty of this as well. This disconnect occurs when we fail to realize that reflection can help students demonstrate high-order thinking, while possibly sharing their learning—perhaps when we dedicate five minutes at the end of class for students to share their progress. Reflection can take place wherever, whenever. It can also help us revise and refine our work.

When we consider why we have students reflect during project based learning, it falls into one of two categories. The first category is non-evaluative, as it doesn't connect to specific learning targets; you're trying to get students to think critically about their work. Use prompts, if necessary, and think about fading out those prompts to promote independence (think gradual release). Here are some examples:

- What additional questions do you have about this topic?
- What strengths can you identify in your work?

- What are you most proud of?

- How could you improve your work?

- What would you do differently next time?

- What connections can you make between _____ and your previous experiences?

- How has this new learning changed your thinking?

The second category is more evaluative, as it connects to specific learning targets and could potentially fall under Step 2 instead of Step 3. Here, use prompts to draw out information from students when you want to ascertain whether or not they have learned the material. Use these reflections for assessment purposes and possibly grades. Here are three examples.

Example 1. Students are engineering solar-powered cars, and you want to make sure students understand how their cars harness the sun's power to propel (or not propel) their vehicles. Ask them: Using academic vocabulary, explain all the steps that had to take place for your car to transform the sun's energy into motion. If your car isn't working, include when and why the breakdown occurred and what you're going to do to fix it.

Example 2. Students are tasked with designing their own businesses, which they will pitch to local entrepreneurs for feedback. You want to make sure students understand what a quality pitch involves. After each student's first pitch, ask: Reflect upon your pitch, one component at a time. Based on the feedback you received, what will you change when you pitch again?

Example 3. Students are tasked with finding and solving a schoolwide problem. You want to make sure students understand empathy and the ways in which they have to consider all stakeholders when tackling their problem. Toward the middle of the project, ask: One stakeholder at a time, explain your strategy for addressing their wants, needs, and perspectives.

For both types of reflection, ask students to reflect in multiple ways, such as through written reflections, blogging, videos, or discussions. During and after the reflection process, make time for them to improve on their work.

Publishing

Much like reflection, publishing doesn't just come at the end of a project, as it should mimic as closely as possible what we do as adults. As we state in *Hacking Project Based Learning*:

> Throughout any given project, students can: write blog posts, work on a website, produce videos, leverage social media, etc. Students may make their work public throughout the duration of a project to: obtain audience feedback, promote their work, provide self-motivation, or because multiple steps are involved and they have chosen to publish after each one (e.g., creating multiple videos as opposed to one). In other instances, students may work away on their project throughout the duration of a PBL unit and finally hit publish once everything is complete.

Here are three ways in which you can use publishing as part of project based learning. These ways are not mutually exclusive.

Example 1. Use publishing to document the process. Have students continuously film their work in progress, and every Friday, ask them to publish a more polished video that documents their process (which helps them to obtain feedback and reflect on their work).

Example 2. Use publishing as the project's final product. If students are raising awareness for an endangered animal, like the bald eagle, ask them to publish an original song toward the end of the project and then promote it via social media to raise awareness.

Example 3. Use publishing for sharing. If students are using the school's outdoor classroom to grow vegetables and explore the idea of farm to table, ask them to create presentations to share what they've learned with other students, families, and outside experts, possibly at a community exhibition or other event.

STUDENT CHOICE NEEDS TO BE MORE THAN LETTING STUDENTS DECIDE WHERE THEY CAN COPY AND PASTE THEIR WORK.

Approach the publishing platform with intentionality. It's easy to fall into the trap of crying "differentiation" or "student choice" when students are allowed to present what they've learned however they want, such as via PowerPoint, Prezi, or an infographic. But student choice needs to be more than letting students decide where they can copy and paste their work.

The alternative approach is for students to decide on their publishing platform during the thick of the project, with flexibility to change along the way. Rather than choices being made based on what's cool or easily accessible, ask students to make their choices based on what they are trying to accomplish. For example, if students are looking to make a difference in the community, social media is a viable option. If they're looking to influence other students, they can potentially use the morning announcements or hang up posters around the school. The true differentiation occurs as students or groups of students carve out their own paths to meet their learning goals. While technologies and mediums are part of this process, they are not the differentiation in and of themselves.

REVISE YOUR NARRATIVE

Now let's take a look at a revised version of the project narrative, written from the point of view of a teacher who is well-versed in project based learning. The three paragraphs coincide with the three steps of backward design. (Chapter 6 contains an in-depth look at materials mentioned in the second paragraph.)

> In two weeks, I know I have to teach animal adaptations. And because this topic is so broad, and because I want my students to learn at a deeper level, I'll begin the planning process with two High Impact Takeaways that connect to the academic standards that will serve as the project's main focus. The two High Impact Takeaways are: (1) All animals have basic needs that must be met, and (2) All animals must adapt to their surroundings. With these two High Impact Takeaways in mind, the project will follow a Problem Track in which students, working in small groups, must adopt an endangered animal and take action to help it survive. The Umbrella Question will be "How can the animals be helped?" because the project isn't just about how the animals can help themselves through adaptations, but also how we as a class can help them. For a relevant title, we'll call the project Angry Animals (instead of Angry Birds). Finally, along with High Impact Content related to animal adaptations, I'll filter in Supporting Content related to the environment and also literacy, as students will regularly reflect upon their work through blogging.
>
> I'll introduce the project to the students by first having them watch a current newsclip on endangered animals. Then I'll distribute and review with students: (1) a one-pager with the project's directions, (2)

interactive directions in which each group will document their journeys as they help their animals, (3) one Progress Assessment Tool per group and one per student, and (4) a folder for students to organize all project-related materials. All project-related materials will be posted on the project's website. The Progress Assessment Tool will contain the project's learning targets, which deal with animal adaptations, and it will also include the learning targets related to environment and literacy. Each learning target will be accompanied by a few bullet points that clarify what students need to do to score a 3. In all, there will be about eight learning targets. As students work through their projects, I'll continuously make sure they're following directions with the help of their interactive directions. At the same time, I'll put the structures in place for them to always be receiving feedback in relation to the learning targets on the Progress Assessment Tool. This feedback can be teacher-to-student, student-to-student, and student-to-self. Finally, because students will be partially assessed as a group, I'll want to make sure each individual learns the necessary information. So, at the conclusion of the project there will be a culminating test with questions that connect to the project's learning targets (not the project itself). So this test doesn't come as a surprise, I'll mention it at the bottom of the project's directions. This test, along with the ongoing feedback and individual blog posts, should tell me who knows what.

After the students receive their project-related materials and form their groups, but before they dive into the actual project, we'll spend a few classes building student background knowledge on the topic of animal adaptations. Once the background knowledge has been built, a good amount of time will be spent on students, in groups, working through their projects and interactive directions. However, about once every two days, I'll ask them to stop their work so I can engage them in a lesson on animal adaptations. My science textbook has ten activities on the topic, and based on what I know about my students, I plan to use five of them. Rather than having students actually use their textbooks, I'll extract these five lessons and refine and rebrand them as part of the project. Along with these five activities, I'll use science magazines and YouTube for three more, and I'll also make sure to be flexible and filter in additional lessons based on students' needs. Some of these lessons may relate to animal adaptations, and some of them may relate more to project-related tasks, such as how to create and publish an e-book to raise awareness for an endangered animal.

Planning a project based learning experience is more complex than planning a project. But once you start to transition to project based learning, you never go back. We'll end with three tips, from the PBL Paralysis graphic, which should help.

OVERCOMING PBL PARALYSIS
3 TIPS TO TRANSITION FROM A PROJECT TO A PROJECT BASED LEARNING EXPERIENCE

It can be intimidating to start the planning process with nothing at all. So start by tackling the components every project has in common:

- Title
- High Impact Content & Supporting Content
- High Impact Takeaways
- Umbrella Question
- Learning targets
- Progress Assessment Tool, etc.

Once these components have been determined, the rest of the planning should be that much easier.

Think about what you will distribute to students for every project:

- One-page directions (one-sided)
- Interactive directions
- Progress Assessment Tool
- Folder for all project-related papers
- Digital hub (website or learning management system) that contains all project-related resources.

Working with all of these common denominators creates a routine for teachers, students, and families, and helps to alleviate what could otherwise be a chaotic process. These common denominators are explored in-depth in Chapter 6.

Build on top of your most recent project, which should be your best. As teachers, for every project we designed, we referenced our most recent project and then improved upon its structure while sometimes asking for student feedback. As a result, we were never starting with a blank slate, and our work was always getting better.

FINAL THOUGHTS

Finally, we caution you against overplanning in isolation. We recently did a podcast with Elisabeth Bostwick, an instructional coach and author. During the podcast, she talked about the myth—but reality—of educators sitting around a giant table, "perfectly planning" their PBL unit, delivering it to students, and then hoping for the best. Not surprisingly, this scene resembles our early days of project based learning. The problem: When we take this approach to planning, we're leaving out our most valuable stakeholders, our students. Don't hesitate to give your students a voice during the learning *and* planning process. If you're transitioning to project based learning, communicate to students (and possibly families) how your instruction is changing and why, while continuously asking for their feedback. This way, everyone is moving together toward project based learning, as opposed to it being something that is "done to students."

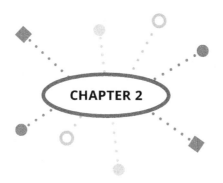

REAL QUESTION:

How Do I Get Grades?

*If we remove the label, we encourage students
to see themselves simply as learners.*
— STARR SACKSTEIN, EDUCATION BLOGGER AND
AUTHOR OF *HACKING ASSESSMENT*

THE QUESTION WE hear most frequently is, "How do I get grades?" And understandably so. If our students are going to be engaged in a month-long project, our gradebook needs to have *something* to show for it. Right?

Ross: As an administrative intern at Lower Macungie Middle School in Macungie, Pennsylvania, I was given a copy of *Fair Isn't Always Equal* by Rick Wormeli. For almost a year, the book sat on a shelf, collecting dust. It wasn't until I left the classroom and became an assistant principal that I decided to read it. I was floored by the ways in which the author's ideas and philosophies disagreed with my own. And as I soon found out, there were also glaring discrepancies between my practices and the research in several other books on assessment and grading. In fact, I had committed many of the classic mistakes cited in these books: averaging grades, grading group work, and forcing students to adhere to strict deadlines when handing in assignments.

So, what went wrong?

I waited too long to read the book. Additionally, the majority of educators never receive formal professional learning on assessment and grading. But we must educate ourselves beyond our classroom experiences. If we don't, we're doing our students a disservice by potentially grading them the same way we were graded when we were students, which, of course, can be problematic. It also means that we'll make the same mistakes that others may be making at our school.

We start by examining our grading habits, keeping in mind the difference between assessment and grading. That difference is the first step toward improving our practices. We need to make sure we don't use those two terms interchangeably when speaking with educators, students, and families.

In short, whereas the goal of assessment is to improve student learning (think: feedback), grading (or a grade) is generally used to evaluate the current level of performance. From the student's point of view, assessment says, "I want to help you," while grading says, "I want to judge you." We don't work well when we feel like we're being judged.

REAL ANSWERS:

DETERMINE WHETHER PROJECTS SHOULD BE GRADED

Should projects be graded? Most often, our response to this question is a resounding "No!"

Project based learning experiences should call for a great deal of student critical thinking and creativity, as should the majority of approaches to teaching and learning. Research tells us that the carrot-and-stick method for teaching these types of skills isn't just ineffective, but detrimental. Daniel Pink calls our attention to this problem in his 2009 book, *Drive*—the book that has been, in large part, responsible for countless educators taking on Genius Hour (also referred to as 20 Percent Time and Passion Projects) in their classrooms. The same year Drive was released, Pink gave a TED Talk based on the book *The Puzzle of Motivation* (2009). Here is the take-home point for a segment. This begins at the one-minute, thirty-second mark:

ASSESSMENT SAYS, "I WANT TO HELP YOU," WHILE GRADING SAYS, "I WANT TO JUDGE YOU."

> If-then rewards work really well for those sorts of tasks, where there is a simple set of rules and a clear destination to go to. Rewards, by their very nature, narrow our focus, concentrate the mind; that's why they work in so many cases. ... But for the real candle problem [a problem that requires creative problem solving], you don't want to be looking like this [tunnel vision]. The solution is on the periphery. You want to be looking around. That reward actually narrows our focus and restricts our possibility.

Pink also makes it clear this experiment is not the exception to the rule: "What's interesting about this experiment is that it's not an aberration. This has been replicated over and over again for nearly forty years."

Regarding grades as a whole, Alfie Kohn has repeatedly written about their harmful nature. In his seminal article "The Case Against Grades" from *Educational Leadership* (2011), he lists three research-based conclusions: grades tend to diminish students' interest in whatever they're learning, grades create a preference for the easiest possible task, and grades tend to reduce the quality of students' thinking. Kohn goes on to claim, "If nourishing [students'] *desire* to learn is a primary goal for us, then grading is problematic by its very nature."

Looking back on our work as classroom teachers, we can draw a straight line from Pink's work to our misuse of grades as the carrot and the stick. The more we engaged our students in project based learning, the more we realized that grading the actual project was not only unnecessary, but potentially harmful. And, as Kohn tells us, "Sometimes it's only after grading has ended that we realize just how harmful it's been."

GIVE FEEDBACK WITHOUT GRADES

If not grades, then what? The short answer is feedback without grades.

As classroom teachers, we found that grading student work sometimes took up an entire weekend. And typically, come Sunday night, student work contained feedback and a grade. Little did we know, this was not time well spent.

When you hand back feedback and a grade, students first look at the grade. Second, they look at the grades of their classmates. Third, they ignore the feedback. If you truly want to move students from where they are to where they need to be, feedback in the absence of grades is the answer.

Feedback needs to tell the learner three things:

- **Where they are:** The student's current abilities.

- **Where they need to go:** The student's current abilities in relation to success criteria and hitting the learning target(s) for which they are striving.

- **How to get there:** What the student needs to do to work toward achieving success criteria and hitting the target(s).

Three additional points that touch on common mistakes:

Students must have a chance to respond to feedback (actionable), or it's not feedback. In other words, we shouldn't tell students how they could improve upon their Chapter 3 work but then immediately move on to Chapter 4 without allowing them to revisit Chapter 3. This would be equivalent to one of our supervisors informing us how we could better ourselves without giving us the opportunity to do so.

Feedback must directly and clearly relate to what students are trying to achieve (goal-oriented), or it's not feedback. These goals, which often come in the form of the previously discussed learning targets and success criteria, are feedback's "where we need to go." Without these destinations, along with clear strategies as to how to get there, students will likely be lost, and we've wasted our time.

Helping students determine "how to get there" is different than asking students to follow scripted directions. If students are attempting to eradicate a fungus from the school garden, we wouldn't hand them a fungicide and tell them to apply it twice daily. Instead, we may ask them if they have researched common ways to treat fungus and help them to decide on an option to get started.

SUPPORT STUDENT SELF-ASSESSMENT

When learners feel safe and supported, feedback can flow freely and generally takes on three forms: teacher-to-student, student-to-student, and student-to-self. While all three will occur at one point or another, when you're dealing with assessment, student self-assessment should be your endgame with the purpose of students owning the learning as much as possible.

As John Hattie tells us in *Visible Learning for Teachers* (2012):

> The greatest effects on student learning occur when teachers become learners of their own teaching, and when students become their own teachers. When students become their own teachers, they exhibit the self-regulatory attributes that seem most desirable for learners (self-monitoring, self-evaluation, self-assessment, self-teaching).

Based on our experiences, four components are necessary for student self-assessment to become the norm, while also making sure feedback connects to what students need to learn. The first three components involve the three columns of the previously discussed Progress Assessment Tool.

- **Learning targets (left column):** Student-friendly standards.

- **Success criteria (middle column):** What it looks like when students hit each target.

- **Feedback (right column):** Feedback in relation to where the student is on the continuum of hitting each learning target by satisfying its success criteria. At some point, students need to learn what feedback is (and is not), and the information from the previous section can help. Also, you can deepen students' understanding of feedback by having them analyze authentic examples and nonexamples from Amazon reviews, album and movie reviews, blog post comments, and previous work that's been assessed. The Chapter 5 PBL

Paralysis graphic details a six-step process for having students uncover the features of effective collaboration. You can easily tweak and use this process when working with students to define feedback. Once students have a solid understanding of feedback, work with them to apply it to their work in progress. This chapter's PBL Paralysis graphic contains two ways we model feedback for students.

- **Protocols (not included in the Progress Assessment Tool):** We also need to set aside class time for student self-assessment through the use of protocols. This time is dedicated to students practicing and applying self-assessment without the pressures of having to simultaneously move forward with their work. Following are five different protocols, some of them making more use of the Progress Assessment Tool than others.

    Goal setting #1. During a project, ask each student to select one to two learning targets that stand out as areas for improvement, and give self-feedback for each target, while referencing its success criteria, in each target's respective feedback row in the Progress Assessment Tool. Then, for each target, feedback and success criteria are used to create an improvement plan. This can be mapped out below each target's feedback on the Progress Assessment Tool, in an optional goal-setting column inserted to the right of the feedback column, or on a separate form. Optionally, revisit improvement plans at a later point in time to gauge the level of success.

Goal setting #2. During a project, after providing a considerable amount of feedback, give students time to analyze all the feedback on their Progress Assessment Tool. Ask each student to compartmentalize the feedback into one of three categories: feedback that has been satisfied; feedback that needs satisfying, and the student knows what to do (action steps are recorded below the feedback in a goal-setting column or on a separate form); and feedback that needs satisfying, and the student doesn't know what to do (questions for others are also recorded). Afterward, give students time to start on their action steps while you circle the room, taking care of questions that only require brief answers.

Differentiated lesson. While students are in the middle of a lesson, which may or may not be connected to project based learning, and before they split off into centers, call their attention to the lesson's learning target and success criteria. Give them time to determine whether or not they can hit the target. Depending on the content, this task may be completed orally, mentally, on a digital discussion board, on a small dry-erase board, in a notebook, or on a worksheet. After this check for understanding, ask them to decide whether or not they require additional support. Differentiate the centers accordingly.

Umbrella Question journaling. Journals can be created on paper or digitally, as long as each student has a designated location for the work. Throughout a project, students compose written responses to the project's Umbrella Question. Those responses should become more insightful as the project progresses. Schedule the responses (e.g., every Friday) or allow students to complete them whenever they see fit. Students can also use their journals to create mind maps that connect all project-related content, with the Umbrella Question in the center as the project's main idea. Other options include drawings, sketchnotes, and videos, all of which students can use to connect their learning to the Umbrella Question while self-assessing their own progress.

Reflection. We can also get our students into the habit of self-assessment and reflection by giving them prompts, which don't necessarily have to connect to learning targets. Use any of the seven prompts from Chapter 1. Use this option as a non-threatening entry point for students who aren't used to talking about their own work. Meanwhile, use reflection questions that more closely connect to specific learning targets for evaluative purposes.

For all protocols, if students struggle to work independently, provide teacher or peer assistance.

OVERCOMING PBL PARALYSIS
2 WAYS TO MODEL FEEDBACK FOR STUDENTS

GRADUAL RELEASE

TEACHER-TO-STUDENT

STUDENT-TO-SELF

Instead of starting with student-to-self feedback, start with teacher-to-student. Over time students can take the lead in these conversations. Then, filter in more and more student-to-student, followed by more and more student-to-self. This way, students are prepared for student-to-self by first learning how to give feedback from both their teacher and their peers.

STUDENT-TO-STUDENT

EXPLICIT MODELING

This activity is usually done as an entire class or in small groups. It involves the teacher and students working together to assess a piece of work:

- Choose a piece of work, either authentic student work or teacher-generated. Special consideration can be given to using exemplars or work with common mistakes, if appropriate.
- Assess the work by working through the learning targets, one at a time.
- For each target, discuss the feedback that should be given.
- If the work encompasses many learning targets, it may be best to focus on only a few of them.

SUPPORT PEER ASSESSMENT

While you want students to always be building their capacity to self-assess, you still need to set aside time for peer assessment, as it can be invaluable for students to hear multiple perspectives of their work. The level of our work also tends to elevate when we immerse ourselves in the work of others while giving feedback.

In *Peer Feedback in the Classroom* (2017), Starr Sackstein explains how peer assessment empowers students to be experts:

> Every student has the potential to be an expert.... By giving students the responsibility to share their expertise with one another, we are engaging them in the highest level of learning: asking them to teach.... There is no longer a need for teachers to be the only experts in the room.

For any given situation, base the form of assessment we ask students to utilize (self- or peer assessment), and its respective activity, on students' abilities and needs. As students become familiar with our protocols, they can choose which one to use, or they can use protocols of their own.

Here are five protocols to support peer assessment.

Peer conferences. Students meet and give each other feedback pertaining to the project's learning targets. Feedback can be given orally or written in each target's respective feedback row in the Progress Assessment Tool. (In the next chapter, we'll explore explicit steps—gather, give, go—that can be used for these conferences.) Throughout any project, schedule peer conferences on a regular basis, such as once a week for twenty minutes. You want to strike a balance between the same pairs always forming to encourage continuity, and students meeting with new partners to encourage fresh perspectives. For group projects, you want a mix of group members meeting with each other and with those from other groups.

Gallery walk. Students put their projects on display, and everyone silently views and gives feedback on each other's work, oftentimes on a feedback form that is next to the project. If you want the feedback to be more focused, the teacher or students can ask for feedback related to specific learning targets. If the project in progress isn't entirely self-explanatory, have the students leave a written explanation next to it (individual projects), or have one group member stay back to explain the work (group projects). Afterward, give students time to process their feedback and plan action steps.

Fishbowl. If you have students who demonstrate strengths in asking questions, reflecting, and providing feedback, ask them to model for the class. The students on the inside of the circular fishbowl model the intended practice, and the rest of the class, on the outside, listens and takes notes. At certain points, roles can be reversed, giving more students an opportunity to be in the fishbowl. Afterward, the class discusses what worked well. For project based learning, a few options include: students from different groups in the fishbowl, giving each other feedback, or an entire group in the fishbowl, openly discussing their project. For more examples demonstrating the fishbowl protocol for peer assessment, see the Times 10 Publication book *The Startup Teacher Playbook* (2021) by Michelle Blanchet and Darcy Bakkegard.

Braintrust. In *Creativity, Inc.* (2014), Ed Catmull tells us all about Pixar's Braintrust meetings. He describes them "As Pixar's version of peer review, a forum that ensures we raise our game—not by being prescriptive but by offering candor and deep analysis." While Pixar uses its Braintrust for peer feedback during filmmaking, we can have a classroom Braintrust for feedback during projects. An individual or group presents the project in progress to the rest of the class, and the class gives oral feedback. These meetings are powerful when presenters are honest about what is or isn't working; candid feedback focuses on the work, not the presenters; and the presenters are open to feedback. "Inside the Pixar Braintrust," an excerpt from *Creativity, Inc.*, can be found at realpbl.com/resources.

Receiving feedback. In *Thanks for the Feedback* (2014), Douglas Stone and Sheila Heen explain why pull (receiving feedback) beats push (giving feedback): "If the receiver isn't willing or able to absorb the feedback, then there's only so far persistence or even skillful delivery can go." So, we also need to work with students (and ourselves) on receiving feedback. This starts with students being conscious of their thoughts and actions when they're on the receiving end. Try discussing and roleplaying with students when they're most likely to accept or reject feedback.

For extensions of these strategies on peer assessment, we can refer to the section on Thinking Routines in Chapter 4 and the section on Collaboration in Chapter 5.

Throughout a project, regularly schedule time for self- and peer assessment. These sessions will help to establish a culture of feedback and will also help promote true collaboration through interdependence, with everyone being mutually dependent on each other to improve their work and to move forward as learners.

USE FORMAL ASSESSMENTS

Sometimes feedback alone won't cut it, and you'll need a bit more to determine who got what. This "bit more" can take the shape of more formal assessments, such as quizzes or tests that assess students' abilities to hit the projects' learning targets. Ideally, these assessments would be formative in nature (not graded), with their data being used to drive instruction. We understand, however, that grades are sometimes needed.

Here are four occasions in which a formal assessment could be necessary.

Your Progress Assessment Tool is busted. There will be instances in which you've just begun a project and you realize that your Progress Assessment Tool is busted and in need of major revisions. There will also be instances in which the project is near its end, and you don't have enough information to confidently conclude who knows what. In our experiences, both of these problems were more likely to occur when we were PBL rookies, still learning how to make it happen effectively, or when it was the first time we were rolling out a project, and it was impossible to foresee all the twists and turns we would encounter. So if and when you find yourself in the dark regarding whether students learned what they were supposed to learn, don't be afraid to issue a formal assessment or two.

Group work. While the majority of projects are completed as groups, Rick Wormeli in *Fair Isn't Always Equal* (2018) tells us, "Group grades don't reflect an individual student's achievement or growth and therefore can't be used to document progress, provide feedback, or inform instructional decisions regarding individual students." Also, these grades do not account for the fact that each student within any particular group will develop different under-standings at different rates. In other words, no two students are the same. Truly, we are doing our students a disservice if we are allowing their knowledge (or lack thereof) of certain content to be masked by others. Also, we're sure most of us can recall at least one story in which we suffered as a result of having to work in a group.

As teachers, one strategy we tried was the jigsawing of a project, with each student in a group being held accountable and graded on a specific, unique portion of the group's work. While this approach can help to tidy up and streamline "who does what," for jigsawing to be defensible, we also need to make sure students can't skate by without 1) actually collaborating, and 2) having to immerse themselves in and be assessed on valuable aspects of the project. What also worked for our students was group work in which groups and individuals received feedback (teacher, peer, and self-feedback) all along the way, and then at the conclusion of the project, each student was formally assessed. For group and individual projects, we can also formally assess each student at a few specific points throughout, such as when a project reaches a "hinge point" when there is a clear shift in content.

So you want to be progressive! *Ross:* During my first few years in the classroom, I was constantly challenging myself to be more progressive by always exposing students to teaching and learning experiences that were new to me. While most of us do believe we should always be moving forward, students and families don't always associate the latest and greatest with what meets their needs. As one of my mentors reminded me, "Students don't care if it's new to you. What matters is that it works for them." While assessing strictly based on a project may feel progressive and forward-thinking for the teacher, more traditional techniques (such as a paper-and-pencil quiz) can be incorporated to assist students in feeling comfortable with project based learning, especially when they are inexperienced with this type of learning. In addition, we have found that the use of more traditional assessments helps ease concerns with families by providing a balance for those who may be wary of the progressive nature of project based learning.

You gave too much help. Ultimately, you want to know what students can accomplish independently, and their grades should reflect this individual achievement. While group work can mask what students are capable of doing, so can too much teacher support, or too much assistance from parents, guardians, or siblings. So, if you find yourself giving students too much help during their projects, at least one formal assessment may be necessary to determine what they can do on their own.

DESIGN A FORMAL ASSESSMENT

Here are ten questions to consider when designing a project based learning assessment.

For each question:

1. For each learning target assessed, is it assessed to the same depth to which it has been taught? In other words, are your questions mirroring your instruction? Webb's Depth of Knowledge can help.

2. For questions that assess higher-order thinking, have you considered grading with a rubric as opposed to marking it right or wrong?

3. Could students get the question correct or get a high score without understanding the material, or could they understand the material but somehow score poorly? In other words, will the question provide valid data?

For the assessment:

1. Do questions relate to the project's learning targets, while potentially omitting content that isn't emphasized as heavily during the project and could possibly be assessed informally?

2. For each learning target, does the assessment give students enough of an opportunity to demonstrate

mastery while not asking for an excessive amount of information/answers?

3. Based on a student's answers, could you determine the level of achievement for each assessed learning target (and then differentiate accordingly)?

4. To the greatest extent possible, are you reporting out student achievement for each learning target (e.g., standards-based grading), as opposed to combining everything into one score (e.g., percentage grades)?

Context:

1. Are you formatively assessing throughout the project (and then differentiating accordingly), as opposed to waiting until the end to formally check for understanding?

2. If this is a formative assessment, are you using its data to drive instruction without issuing grades? If this is a summative assessment, are you issuing grades while still maybe allowing for students to be retaught and regraded on content with which they're struggling?

3. From the beginning of the project, do students know when formal assessments will take place? Consider incorporating this information into the project's directions. For example, at the bottom of some of our directions, we used to include: "At the end of the project, there will be a culminating test." We can also insert assessments at certain hinge points. Formal assessments can counteract those who claim, "But my students won't want to do the project if it's not graded!"

Also, we generally prefer open-ended questions, as students are usually already so consumed with their PBL work that distracting them with a performance task (the term sometimes used to refer to shorter, more structured projects that tend to focus on only a few academic standards) could take too much time and emphasis away from the project (unless the performance task feels like a natural extension of the project rather than a detour). If an assessment comes toward the middle or end of the project, we have found that students appreciate the change of pace provided by open-ended questions. You just need to make sure students' literacy skills, or lack thereof, don't interfere with their ability to communicate what they know.

At some point, perhaps separate from the PBL unit, you can also review the content in the same format as it will most likely be presented on your state test. While you certainly don't want to teach to the test, you do want your students to feel comfortable and prepared.

GRADE THE PROJECT, IF NECESSARY

If you want or need to grade the actual project, here's what we recommend.

Use the Progress Assessment Tool, and add a fourth column between Success Criteria and Feedback. For each learning target, this column should contain the numbers or letters used on your school's report card (e.g., 4, 3, 2, 1 for standards-based grading or A, B, C, D for traditional grading). Throughout the project, as you give students feedback, you can also tell them their current grade for each learning target while potentially relying on how these grades are described on the report card. Then, when the project concludes, assign them their final grades, one per learning target.

Hopefully, at this point your job is done, as combining all of the grades into one could obscure students' strengths and areas for growth. But if an overall grade is needed, for both standards-based or traditional grading, this grade is derived from the median or mode of all the grades. You can also use your professional judgment to ensure that the overall grade is indicative of the learning.

Additionally, if you will weight some grades more than others by counting them more than once, communicate this information to students when you distribute the Progress Assessment Tool. Either way, you always use the median or mode, but never the mean, as this method could potentially allow for one outlying grade (high or low) to have too much influence on the overall grade.

Finally, for traditional grading, if a percentage score is needed, correlate the overall letter grade with a percentage grade (e.g., A is equivalent to 95 percent, B is equivalent to 85 percent).

FINAL THOUGHTS

Pablo Picasso said, "Learn the rules like a pro so you can break them like an artist." And we believe this quote applies to teachers throwing out grades in lieu of feedback. Defensible assessment and grading practices are the rules, and getting rid of grades is equivalent to breaking them. But if we break the rules before we have an informed understanding of what they are, we may end up doing more harm than good. So while we are proponents of doing away with grades, we still believe a solid understanding of assessment and grading is a prerequisite to going gradeless.

The goals are to have the courage to provide feedback throughout projects to promote learning, consider formal assessments if necessary, and work toward minimizing the focus on grades to the greatest extent possible.

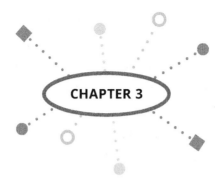

CHAPTER 3

REAL QUESTION:

How Do I Conference with Students?

*Learning to confer well is ultimately the real difference
between a good teacher and a great one.*
— LUCY CALKINS, MARY EHRENWORTH, AND LAURIE
PESSAH, AUTHORS OF *LEADING WELL*

A S ADMINISTRATORS, WE value one-on-one conversations with teachers. Each of these connections allows us to learn more about the teacher as a person and as a professional. *Erin:* During one meeting, a teacher new to inquiry and project based learning shared with me some of the challenges arising in his classroom.

> **Teacher:** Last week didn't go very well. When I collected their assignments, a lot of the groups had the work all wrong.

Erin: I'm sorry; I know that was probably frustrating. When we met previously, we discussed conferring. When you conferred with students during the week, what did you find out?

Teacher: As I checked in around the room, I knew some of the groups were off-base.

Erin: What did you do?

Teacher: I checked in with them, but it was hard. There were a lot of kids. I also didn't want to ruin the inquiry by saying too much.

This honest exchange, shared here with explicit permission, unearthed two clear teaching points for me as a leader: 1) The teacher was unsure of the purpose of a conference, and 2) The teacher was unsure how to efficiently use conferring to promote learning. This teacher is not alone. Almost any time we talk with a group about feedback and conferring, we encounter questions about the structure and function of a conference.

REAL ANSWERS:

USE CONFERENCES AS A CONDUIT FOR FEEDBACK

When our students are in the throes of a project, they require ongoing support and guidance. As discussed in the previous chapter, student self-assessment followed by peer assessment is ideal. But, at the same time, we need to model the feedback process for students if we expect them to own it. Even when our students do own it, teacher feedback is still valuable and we should give it with intentionality. A leisurely walk around the room to check in on student work will not suffice. Your greatest influence is in the interactions that take place while students are working on their projects.

Feedback, which serves as the crux of these interactions, is one of the most impactful strategies when it comes to improving student learning. And we know that receiving timely, specific feedback helps learners make progress toward their goals. In Chapter 2, we touched on this idea when we discussed students having a chance to respond to feedback. In the article "Seven Keys to Effective Feedback" (2012), Grant Wiggins adds to the conversation with this excerpt on feedback being timely:

> A great problem in education, however, is untimely feedback. Vital feedback on key performances often comes days, weeks, or even months after the performance— think of writing and handing in papers or getting back results on standardized tests. As educators, we should work overtime to figure out ways to ensure that students get more timely feedback and opportunities to use it while the attempt and effects are still fresh in their minds.

During project based learning, this type of feedback is typically exchanged during individual or group conferences. Using the 5 Ws followed by the how, let's explore what these conferences look like. (As a warning for our Type A readers, the 5 Ws appear out of order.)

CONSIDER THE 5 WS OF CONFERENCES

What

More than anything else, a conference is a conversation. When implemented well, you take on a conversational tone, which encourages a natural give-and-take between individuals.

Based on our experiences, conferences during project based learning should:

- Build relationships
- Be conversational in nature
- Follow a predictable structure
- Ensure that students are acquiring the desired learning
- Assist in clarifying potential misconceptions
- Gauge how students are feeling about the overall learning experience

Why

Feedback is most effective when it is individualized, and conferences can make this happen. When you establish trust, everyone involved feels safe sharing and receiving feedback. Consistent conferring can further cement that trust. Developing routines promotes student comfort while increasing their willingness to engage in the feedback loop.

When fewer people are in a conversation, you increase opportunities for individuals to share their thinking and questions. One-on-one and small-group conferences are ideal. For example, after moving around the room and doing a general check in, a teacher could announce to the class, "I notice that many of you are not effectively engineering the base of your structure. Please be sure you are testing your base." While this statement is efficient, and a few of the groups may revisit their work, this piece of feedback can be lost on many students. The results will probably be far more dramatic if the teacher instead visits with each group, specifically highlights the functional part of their structure and challenges them to think more critically about a specific obstacle.

Who

Conferences take place with individuals or groups.

Individuals. One major benefit of individual meetings is student willingness to open up. The downside, however, is the implications on timing; meeting with thirty individuals takes longer than meeting with ten groups. To make your individual conferences more efficient, utilize a set structure for your conferences (detailed later in this chapter). This structure helps develop a predictable rhythm for everyone involved.

Even during group projects, because everyone learns in a unique way, you may want to set aside time to conference with individual students. Here, it helps if every student has their own Progress Assessment Tool. Also, check for individual understanding through formative assessments, such as entrance or exit tickets, one-minute elevator pitches, or by asking reflection questions that call for individuals to make connections between their work and the project's learning targets.

Groups. Group conferences are typical during group projects. Group work helps to expedite our conferences because we have fewer projects to track. In a class of thirty students, we may decide to break the students into ten groups. We generally prefer groups of three because teams are small enough for everyone to be busy, but large enough to keep going if someone is absent. Of course, group size can vary based on the nature of the project.

Even during individual projects, there may be times when we conference with students in small groups. One instance may be when common themes emerge among individual work, such as when multiple students are working on a similar task at the same time. Another instance may be when several students need support with the same concept.

When

We recommend approaching independent work time with an idea of who we're going to confer with and why, while leaving wiggle room should additional needs arise. These decisions can be made based on such factors as students' needs, conference notes, assessment data, or wanting to meet with specific students (or all students) a certain number of times per week.

Before you start to confer, give students a few minutes to get settled and situated and, during this time, encourage them by objectively announcing their actions (e.g., "Three groups are already collaborating. Several students have gotten out their Progress Assessment Tools. Jamie is conducting research."). In between conferences, leave students alone, giving them time and space to work; compliment their work; address pressing matters; answer questions that can be briefly answered; and facilitate conversations or listen in on conversations to get a sense of where students are with their work and where they're headed. During these conversations, if you feel students need assistance, prompt them with probing questions that don't give away too much.

Optionally, toward the beginning of independent work, post the day's conference schedule for all to see. If a conference schedule is posted, students may wait until their scheduled time to meet with you. However, at times, students will want to schedule a conference. To meet these needs, for each day, add two to three "pop-up" conference slots. If these slots aren't filled, use the time to follow up on previous meetings, or meet with more students.

Where

In most cases, conferring should occur in the students' workspace, not yours. Standing or leaning over your learners can be intimidating and uncomfortable. Think about ways you can blend in.

When students are on the floor, join them. When they are at a table, find an extra chair to use.

Carl Anderson (2018) shares reasons why we should meet students where they are:

- Because students feel safer in their own space

- Because students have access to their own materials

- Because nearby students can overhear and learn from the conference

Anderson also says that conferring at a designated conference table may be preferable because you can have access to the materials you need to support student learning. Your conferring table can be centrally located among students for classroom management purposes.

How

An effective conference requires an effective routine. Each of your conferences will differ based on the needs of your learners, and following a set structure will help you make sure all learners' needs are met. Additionally, we recommend that each conference last about five minutes, give or take a minute or two. A structure will also help you in meeting this "requirement."

While meeting with students, we first gather information about their current progress. Then we give them something new. And finally, we get the students ready to go do new work. We adapted this structure from *The Art of Teaching Writing* (Calkins, 1994).

ADOPT A CONFERENCE STRUCTURE

Gather information

There is not much worse than receiving feedback that feels completely off-base, as if the feedback provider has no clue what we've been working on (or who we are and what we believe in). In order to provide meaningful feedback that takes students where you want them to go, first establish where students are. Do this by asking questions that help you familiarize yourself with the current state of their project.

At the beginning of a conference, get your students talking. The project's learning targets will drive most of your conferences, so the questions you ask can prompt students to make connections between their work and those targets.

- Tell me about [insert learning target]?

- How is [insert part of project] helping you hit [insert learning target]?

- Which learning targets do you think you've hit? Which learning targets are you struggling with?

Much like some of the reflection prompts from Chapter 1, these prompts draw out information from students to help you determine whether they have learned the material.

Keep the Progress Assessment Tool, which contains the project's learning targets, visible during the conference to help make connections between a project and its learning targets. Additionally, if you want students to continuously make those connections, ask them to make their Progress Assessment Tool visible whenever they're working on the project rather than just during conferences. But we caution against overusing the assessment tool, as we don't want it to distract from the work; find a balance based on context.

Based on what you know about your learners, if you think it'll be intimidating to start a conference with such a heavy emphasis on learning targets, begin by taking a less formal tone. You can also choose to take this tone if it's one of your first times discussing a project with an individual or group, and you want a bigger picture as to what their work involves. Prompts you can use include:

- How's it going?
- Let's talk about your project!
- What's working? What's not working?

Then, transition into learning targets. As students grow accustomed to the conference structure, chances are they'll make this transition on their own, without your prompting.

Give something new

Individuals of all ages are most productive when they feel they are making progress in work they find meaningful. We all like to feel good about our efforts. Initiate this step by complimenting students on a specific aspect of the current work. This concrete praise prepares students to get the most out of what you're about to say.

As we've mentioned, our experiences indicate that feedback needs to tell the learner three things: where they are, where they need to go, and how to get there. The compliment corresponds with "where they are." Let's break down this step and the two steps that immediately follow.

1. **Where they are:** We compliment the current work.
   We choose our compliment wisely, as it serves as

a starting point for a discussion that involves how the work can be better (Step 2). In other words, to build on students' strengths, Steps 1 and 2 should focus on the same learning target(s). The PBL Paralysis graphic details the science of an effective compliment.

2. **Where they need to go:** Once you gather information about students' progress and compliment their work, provide something new for students to ponder, use, or explore in order to move their work forward. Point out the learning target and its success criteria, contrasting it with the current work. If appropriate, use exemplars. Exemplars are any instance (not necessarily a project) in which a student or someone else hit a learning target by meeting its success criteria.

3. **How to get there:** To bridge the gap between the work and the target(s), work with students to determine next steps. These next steps may involve students hitting the target. Or, if they're far off from meeting its success criteria, work on getting *closer* to the target.

OVERCOMING PBL PARALYSIS
THE SCIENCE OF AN EFFECTIVE COMPLIMENT

To promote growth mindset in our students, we want the compliment to objectively focus on student actions and efforts, not abilities. This way, we intentionally avoid conditioning our students to need us for personal validation.

We don't use such phrases as:

- You're so smart!
- I love how you...
- I like the way you...
- Great job!

Alfie Kohn (2001) explains, "The reason praise can work in the short run is that young children are hungry for our approval. But we have a responsibility not to exploit that dependence for our own convenience." Instead, we simply and objectively name what was done and then add why it's helpful.

Here are three examples:

- I noticed you added more adjectives to your story. These additions will help the story come alive for the reader.
- You positioned the solar panel at approximately a 30 degree angle. This angle maximized its retention of solar energy.
- You took it upon yourself to contact an outside expert for help. Taking this kind of initiative helps you to own your work, and it is a life skill that will be valuable beyond your time in school.

For conferences during Reading and Writing Workshop, to take a less-is-more approach, it is widely recommended that students and teachers find one clear teaching point on which students should focus following the conference. With project based learning, due to its complexities, this idea of "number of teaching points" is more open-ended. Based on what you know about your students, the content, and the project, exercise your professional judgment to determine the size and number of your students' next steps. In some instances, there may be one clear task. In others, there may be a few.

On many occasions, it will feel as if you need to "fix" many potential next steps and an overwhelming number of things. According to Katie Wood Ray in *The Writing Workshop* (2001), questions that can help guide your decision-making include:

- What would help most at this time?
- What would bring quick success?
- What would be a stretch, a risk, or a challenge?
- What is not likely to come up in whole-class instruction?
- What kind of teaching would this student like me to offer?

You may have entered the conference with a strong idea as to what should happen next, or your questions may have uncovered something completely different. Either way, as a result of the conference, students should be able to independently take their next steps and understand how their work is helping them meet or get closer to the designated learning target(s). In other words, the emphasis isn't just on the project, but also on the independent learning that's taking place as a result of the project. If this learning is truly occurring, students should be able to tackle these same targets if and when they're presented in a different context. This is the transfer of learning.

Finally, while your learning targets will hopefully drive the majority of your conferences, be prepared for some conferences that relate to:

- Specific jobs, skills, or tools the majority of students will want to execute or use, but will require assistance. (These jobs, skills, and tools may also be present in the learning targets.)
- Group remediation when students struggle to collaborate.
- Project directions, especially if you were accidentally unclear as to what you wanted students to accomplish.

While you might end up helping with jobs, skills, and tools, avoid remediating student disputes and clarifying directions as much as possible. In both instances, if these problems consistently arise, ask yourself what you can do to proactively avoid these issues altogether. For example, for student disputes, make sure you're proactively teaching students how to collaborate (Chapter 5). For directions, make sure your directions are as clear as possible (Chapter 6), and/or turn the directions into a checklist for students to monitor their own progress more easily.

Be ready to go

A conference is successful if it leaves students more excited than they were before, everyone involved walks away knowing what happens next, and students have a clear understanding of their imminent work. Student work may include researching a question they have not yet explored, reviewing mentor texts to fine-tune their written transitions, or updating a video to more clearly articulate the mission of their public service announcement. To check for student understanding, conclude the conference by asking, "What are you going to do next?" Have students start their next steps in front of you before you officially end the conference.

At the very end of the conference, let students know that at a later time, you're going to check back with them to see how they're doing with their next steps. Then, of course, make good on that promise. This follow-up holds students accountable for their work and helps them feel supported. In a way, you're serving as a safety net in case they struggle with independently taking their next steps. Once you've conditioned students to realize that you will, in fact, be following up, they'll be more likely to actualize the work you expect them to do.

KEEP CONFERENCE RECORDS

For student and teacher reference, we recommend keeping a record of the conference, which can include as little as the conference date and student feedback in the form of next steps. Again, this information can go in the Progress Assessment Tool. For students to own the learning and the assessment process as much as possible, you want them to record this information. If you don't think certain students are capable, or if you think this process will be too burdensome, you can first model this process and then give them more ownership through gradual release of responsibility.

If students are holding onto hard copies of their Progress Assessment Tools and digital versions aren't posted anywhere, you may want to keep your own conference records. These records can help to guide your instruction as you take notice of individual needs and patterns that exist among several students. Use a spreadsheet or table with the following three columns, left to right:

names of students with whom you meet, conference date, and any notes you want to reference in the future. Consider having one conference sheet per individual (individual projects) or one per group (group projects). Here, the individual or group's name goes at the top, followed by two columns: one for dates, one for notes. No matter the style of your form, take the time to briefly jot down notes after each conference.

SUPPORT PEER ASSESSMENT AND SELF-ASSESSMENT

We want students to be able to leverage gather, give, go in order to peer assess and self-assess. Once again, gradual release of responsibility can help. This gradual release process begins with direct instruction, when we take the time to actually teach students what a conference involves while calling attention to the steps and language of gather, give, go along the way. For this teaching to happen within an authentic context, it can take place toward the beginning of the year's first project when you have your first few conferences. Rather than having these conferences in private, facilitate them in front of the rest of the class. Throughout the conferences, periodically pause and explain your thought process to your students. Optionally, as you model, ask the other students to take notes, and use them as a basis for class discussion.

As we mentioned in the previous chapter, you can also teach students how to assess a piece of work by discussing feedback for each of its learning targets. Once students become comfortable being on the receiving end of conferences, they can transition to owning them a bit more by taking the lead. This ownership will become apparent as students start to do the majority of the talking, point out their own strengths and areas for growth, and set their own goals. Instinctively, peer and self-assessment will come next.

Finally, as we teach gather, give, go, we can work with our

students to create materials that outline these three steps. These materials—such as an anchor chart, handouts, and table tents—can be references for everyone involved before, during, and after conferences. They help to make the conference process even more explicit while promoting a common language. If applicable, use the same language and materials across multiple subject areas.

CONSIDER THE THREE TYPES OF CONFERENCES

As previously mentioned, a conference, at its heart, is a conversation. Even when conversations are spontaneous and organic, themes still tend to emerge. We can harness these themes to prepare for and facilitate our conversations more efficiently. Conferences tend to fall into three main categories.

Learning target conference. This type of conference can focus on at least one learning target that has yet to serve as the basis for a meeting, or build on a previous conference by focusing on the same learning targets and gains achieved since a prior meeting. Detailed throughout this chapter, the learning target conference is the most common type of conference.

Student-requested conference. This type of conference focuses on addressing a specific question or concern from an individual or group. While the dialogue is often spontaneous, gather, give, go may still apply. Also, some of these conferences may relate to jobs, skills, tools, group remediation, and project directions.

Reflection conference. Use reflection prompts that connect to specific learning targets (see Chapter 1) to draw out information from students to ascertain whether they have learned the material. Use these reflections for assessment purposes and possibly grades. A reflection conference closely resembles the first step of our conference structure, gather, but you're digging deeper than normal, much like an in-depth interview, and potentially treating this step as its own separate event.

For all three conferences, the gather, give, go structure remains mostly the same. But, depending on the type, you might use different prompts to get the conversation going. Since each conference serves a slightly different purpose, you should also prepare in different ways. Figure 3.1 provides a breakdown of the three main types of conferences and tips for getting started.

	LEARNING TARGET CONFERENCE	STUDENT REQUESTED CONFERENCE	REFLECTION CONFERENCE
GATHER	How is [insert part of project] helping you to hit [insert learning target]? OR Can you show me [insert learning target]?	You said you wanted to discuss...Can you tell me more about that? OR How can I support you?	Using academic vocabulary, explain all of the steps that had to take place for your solar powered car to transform the sun's energy into motion. If your car isn't currently working, include when and why the breakdown occurred and what you're going to do to fix it.
	1. I noticed [insert specific compliment]... 2. I would like to show you... 3. Let's discuss next steps.	1. I heard you say... 2. I would like to show you... 3. Let's discuss next steps.	
GIVE	*Prepare:* We should have a few lessons in our toolbox: one to pull out if the student(s) doesn't demonstrate mastery of the skill, another if the student(s) demonstrates mastery but is capable of deeper application. A final possibility is introducing another skill.	*Prepare:* It can be tricky to prepare for a spur of the moment conference. If students get us their question(s) ahead of time, we can better prepare for the conversation.	*Prepare:* We select our prompt(s) based on the information we want to draw out from students.
GO	What are you going to do next? How do you feel? When we meet again, I would like to see...		

FIGURE 3.1 - Three Types of PBL Conferences   Structure adapted from Calkins, 1994

DEVELOP THE ROUTINE

Developing a sustainable routine requires deliberate practice. Whether you are teaching kindergarten or AP physics, make no assumptions about a student's ability or willingness to engage in productive independent work. In addition, many of your students travel from one classroom to another during the day. It is safe to assume that your expectations may be different from those of your colleagues. Taking the time to prepare students to interact and perform successfully in your classroom requires routines.

A conference schedule can help establish a routine, which means fewer interruptions during conferences. Some students will feel comfortable reading the schedule and waiting until their conference to have their questions addressed. Other students may struggle with this expectation. Students need an understanding of what to do with their questions while you're working with other students. Here are possible solutions:

- If you're using a Progress Assessment Tool, students record each question in the feedback column in the same row as the learning target to which it predominantly applies. If a question doesn't apply to a specific target, it is recorded on the document, outside the table; in an optional goal-setting column; or on a separate form.

- Sticky notes, a journal, or even the margin of the project's directions are all places to jot notes. Students can also leave sticky notes in a designated space on the teacher's desk.

- If students are working digitally, they can use the comment function.

- Students add their questions to a "parking lot" (e.g., designated whiteboard space, wall of sticky notes, or digital message board), which makes them visible to the teacher and other students. This can promote seamless collaboration among individuals and groups.

We recommend defining a specific place for questions in order to save time looking for them during conferences. This common place is especially convenient if students are working in a group. If a specific group member is unavailable or absent during conference time, other members of the group can still facilitate the conversation.

Regardless of the method, take time to rehearse this process with your class. Model a "think aloud" of a situation the students may encounter, and work through the process you want them to follow. This modeling also gives you the opportunity to address the types of questions that warrant a conference interruption (e.g., the Wi-Fi has gone down, a student vomited in the hallway, or Willy Wonka is opening his factory). To promote independence, it's worth documenting this process somewhere in your room. Figure 3.2 is an example of what this documentation could look like.

> PROVIDING STUDENTS WITH FEEDBACK (NOT GRADES) IS POSSIBLY THE MOST IMPORTANT RESOURCE YOU CAN OFFER THEM, AND CONFERENCES ARE THE MAJOR ARTERIES FOR DELIVERING THIS FEEDBACK.

IF...	THEN...
I am looking for confirmation.	Jot your name and concern on a blue sticky note, and place it in the conference column on the board.
We need feedback before moving on.	Jot your names and concern on a red sticky note, and place it in the conference column on the board.
I don't know where to find something.	Check the directions. Ask another student.
Something is broken.	After the current conference, ask to speak with the teacher.
I feel overwhelmed.	Take a break. Place a sticky note on the teacher's desk.
We don't know what to do next.	Check the directions. Check with another group. Send the teacher an email.
We are finished.	Check the directions. Review the Progress Assessment Tool and reflect upon each learning target.

FIGURE 3.2 - Classroom Routine Anchor Chart

If you are working with your youngest learners, you may need to simplify your system. For example, create a green, yellow, and red stoplight. When there are no issues, students are on green. When students need a little support, they move a clothespin with their name on it to yellow. If they are completely stuck, they move their clothespin to red. A similar system can be created with green, yellow, and red cups or cards in the students' workspace. Again, modeling and providing explicit examples of yellow and red concerns will be critical to the success of this method (and also your sanity).

Finally, no matter the ages of your students, think about what materials they will need as they work through their projects. Then, as much as possible, make these materials readily available so they won't have to bother you for them while you're conferring with someone else. What you don't want is for individuals or groups to constantly stop their work, perhaps for lengthy periods, and wait for teacher help before moving on. This wasted time is an obvious sign that you need to take a critical look at the overall systems you have in place.

FINAL THOUGHTS

When we first started to facilitate what we called project based learning, admittedly, we didn't know what to do while our students were working. Most of what we did consisted of:

- Casually walking around, making sure our students followed directions

- Hoping our students would somehow learn the necessary content once they followed these directions

- Bragging to our colleagues about the cool things our students were doing

Providing students with feedback (not grades) is possibly the most important resource you can offer them, and conferences are the major arteries for delivering this feedback. Facilitating a conference is a skill, and just like any skill, it requires practice. We believe this practice is non-negotiable. When you implement a solid structure, connect feedback to learning goals, and continually look to enhance your craft, you're bettering yourself as an educator while at the same time creating a learning environment that will allow your students to thrive—even in your absence.

Over the last few chapters, starting with the Progress Assessment Tool in Chapter 1, we've discussed several assessment options for project based learning. To wrap our heads around the bigger picture, here's a summary of some options:

- Teacher-to-student conferring is our default assessment.

- Throughout a project, we can filter in opportunities for peer assessment, using this technique with more frequency as students grow comfortable with it.

- Self-assessment is our endgame, though it isn't always easy to achieve. Just like peer assessment, students can use this technique with more frequency as they grow comfortable with it.

- The Progress Assessment Tool helps us formalize the assessment process by making it goal-oriented. As much as possible, use it for assessment, not grading.

- Formal formative assessments such as non-graded quizzes can be used during a project to gauge where students are and then drive instruction.

- If a grade is needed, consider using a graded assessment such as a test at the conclusion of a project.

In this chapter, we explored how direct instruction can be infused into conferences with our students. In the next chapter, we'll round out the different ways in which direct instruction can materialize during project based learning.

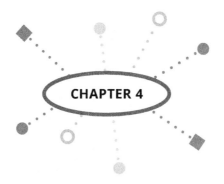

CHAPTER 4

REAL QUESTION:

How Do I Include Direct Instruction?

It's hard to provoke or elicit good thinking from students when there is not much to think about to begin with.
— KARIN MORRISON, RON RITCHHART, AND MARK CHURCH, AUTHORS OF *MAKING THINKING VISIBLE*

ONE BEAUTIFUL THING about project based learning and inquiry is the opportunity for students to uncover new content on their own. Through exploration and problem-solving, children make truly remarkable discoveries, many of which teachers will not foresee. But we can't assume that students will naturally bump into *all* of the information we want them to learn.

Erin: A teacher once told me that he could not bring himself to embrace inquiry because he is "really good" at direct instruction. He believed his ability to tell stories and interact with students was his professional strength. I valued his transparency because it led to an honest conversation that started with a question: Who said project based learning was void of storytelling and direct instruction? After all, students can't think critically about nothing. They have to start somewhere.

Direct instruction, however, has developed negative connotations, especially among fans of project based learning and inquiry. Yet, in *Visible Learning for Teachers*, John Hattie tells us, "One of the more successful methods for maximizing the impact of teaching and enabling teachers to talk to each other about teaching is direct instruction ... often incorrectly confused with transmission or didactic teaching (which it is not)." In reality, didactic teaching relates to slow-paced lectures, and we need a broader definition of direct instruction. Even in a learner-centered classroom, the teacher fills the critical role of content infuser, providing students with new information to ponder, question, challenge, and learn.

When we made the jump to project based learning, we embraced it a bit too much, and for some time, we looked down on direct instruction. Now, thanks to more experience, we know that our students benefit when we strategically leverage direct instruction throughout our PBL units. More specifically, during project based learning, we have found that direct instruction emerges in three distinct ways: proactive, reactive, and learning detours.

REAL ANSWERS:

CONSIDER THE THREE TYPES OF DIRECT INSTRUCTION

Proactive direct instruction

Generally done with the whole class, this instruction can involve:

- Content the majority of students will need as background knowledge to engage in the project

- Content related to common misconceptions

- Content students need to learn, but might not uncover on their own as they work through their projects

- Specific jobs, skills, or tools the majority of students will want to execute or use, but will require assistance

In all instances, ask yourself: "Will the majority of my students be better off if I simply 'feed them' this information ahead of time, or should I make them work for it?" If you think you're going to end up with a struggle that makes students unnecessarily anxious rather than a productive struggle that leads to deep learning, proactively teach the content.

To inform that decision-making, consider what you know about your students (pre-assessments can help), what you know about the content, what you know about the project, and how much time you're willing to dedicate to it. Once you decide content is worth teaching, address it close to the time when students are going to need it: before or toward the beginning of the project, or during the project prior to students bumping into it. This is called just-in-time learning.

If you're going to use a pre-assessment, design it with the

following questions in mind—the first three of which are adapted
from the previous bullet points:

- What background knowledge will your students
  need in order to engage in the project?
- What common misconceptions exist
  among your students?
- What specific jobs, skills, or tools
  will require your assistance?
- What do your students already know,
  and not know, about what you're
  about to study?

> NURTURING
> STUDENTS'
> CURIOSITIES
> SUPERSEDES
> COVERING THE
> CURRICULUM.

- How interested are your students in what you're about
  to study?
- What do you need to know if you're going to assign
  students to groups?

Reactive direct instruction

This is the crux of differentiated instruction, when you are in the
middle of a project and recognize that students need additional support. This instruction, which generally comes in three forms, directly
relates to the conferring we discussed in the previous chapter:

- One-on-one conferring helps you meet a student's
  unique needs.
- Group instruction helps you meet a group's unique
  needs during a group project, or during an individual
  project when several students are demonstrating the
  same need.

- Whole-class instruction can take place when the majority of students are demonstrating the same need.

Most of the time, content will relate to the project's learning targets. However, it may also relate to:

- Specific jobs, skills, or tools the majority of students will want to execute or use, but will require assistance

- Group remediation when students struggle to collaborate

- Project directions, especially if you were accidentally unclear as to what you wanted students to accomplish

Learning detours

If students know what they have to accomplish, they are more likely to take ownership of their learning. Of course, on their way to their goals, they'll probably take their work in directions that include their passions and interests, which may not be encompassed by academic standards. Or students may stumble upon an unanticipated phenomenon or idea. If that happens, you can react in one of two ways. You stifle student curiosity if you reply with, "That's not what we're learning!" but you nurture students' inquiring minds when you allow for them to investigate their questions.

Nurturing students' curiosities supersedes covering the curriculum. As much as possible, allow for these learning detours either during the project or outside of project time during something like Genius Hour. There will be times when a detour is too long or when you feel the learning won't be beneficial. In these cases, it is helpful to have a parking lot for students to store, share, and possibly collaborate over their findings. When students post their thoughts publicly, it validates their thinking while also creating a platform to inspire the ideas of others.

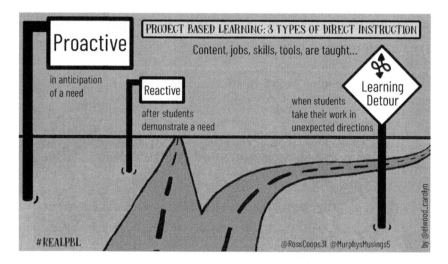

CONSIDER TWO LESSON LENGTHS

Embedding direct instruction into students' in-progress work is a staple of project based learning. Students get started with their tasks and then teachers provide lessons along the way, with students applying what they learn to their work. Maximize student work time by minimizing the length of these lessons, always striving to make them twelve minutes or less. These are mini-lessons.

However, at times, direct instruction may take on a different form and need to last longer, such as forty-five minutes or for an entire instructional period. We call these extended lessons.

We will unpack these two options using the 5 Ws. Then we'll explore the ways you can deliver these lessons. Keep in mind that both types of lessons can occur proactively and reactively. No matter how you teach, you can document the learning by uploading artifacts (e.g., handouts, videos, photographs, photographs of anchor charts) to the project's digital hub for students to access later. (Chapter 6 details how you might create this digital hub.)

Mini-lessons

What. You teach specific and targeted content that you can deliver succinctly, with confidence that your students will apply it to their work.

Why. Mini-lessons allow for brief bursts of new information, while still preserving time for students to practice their craft. You've decided the content isn't worth having students uncover through extended inquiry, possibly due to time constraints or the importance of students acquiring the information as soon as possible.

Who. You might facilitate mini-lessons with the whole class, but because the lessons are short, they don't need to be for all students, all the time. For example, when teaching reactively, you might only include the students who need the instruction.

When. Use mini-lessons when you need them. As often as possible, teach the content just in time so students can apply it to their work either immediately or in the near future.

Where. Since direct instruction will be brief and occur only as needed, make sure your students recognize that something important is happening. Adjust the classroom environment to add to the experience. In an elementary classroom, invite students to the carpet. At this age, students are pretty well-conditioned to know that new learning happens on the carpet. In our secondary classrooms, this can be trickier. If desks are arranged in small groups, ask students to turn their desks to the front of the room. Some teachers have experienced success allowing students to sit on their desks during mini-lessons. Regardless of student age, create a physical stimulus in the environment that will aid with attention and retention.

Extended lessons

What. Teach content that deserves or requires in-depth exploration. However, an extended lesson does not equate to an extended lecture.

Why. Sometimes these types of lessons call for longer amounts of time. For example, students conducting research may need to meet with the librarian to learn how to use the school's online database, or students may need to play around with flashlights and tennis balls to understand the phases of the moon.

Who. Due to the nature of extended lessons, they usually include the entire class. Content can be taught by just about anyone: classroom teachers, special area teachers, administrators, outside experts, or students.

When. Since extended lessons require a substantial pause in student work, you'll want to use them only when they are truly necessary to help students accomplish the project's goals.

Where. Extended lessons can take place anywhere: in a classroom, via virtual learning, outside the school, or in the community. We're redefining the traditional classroom as a learning space, as students can learn beyond the four walls or the digital space.

INTEGRATE MINI-LESSONS

Figure 4.1 shows how the mini-lesson applies to project based learning by breaking a ten- to twelve-minute lesson into five distinct steps.

STEP	PROMPT	CONTENT EXAMPLE	SKILL EXAMPLE
CONNECT TO PRIOR LEARNING (1 minute)	*"During this project we've learned..."*	During this project we've learned how sometimes we need more than just whole numbers to measure what we have.	During this project we've learned how to find credible sources and highlight useful information.
NAME THE TEACHING POINT (1 minute)	*"Today I'm going to teach you..."*	Today I'm going to teach you fraction-related vocabulary: numerator, denominator, proper fractions, equivalent fractions.	Today I'm going to teach you how to reword your research to avoid plagiarism.
TEACH (5 minutes)	*"Let's learn..."*	Let's learn what this vocabulary means - using words, numbers, drawings, and manipulatives.	Let's learn how to take a sentence and reword it while keeping its meaning intact.
ENGAGE STUDENTS (3 minutes)	*"Now it's your turn..."*	Now it's your turn. With your partner, discuss the significance of all four terms. I'll circle around and chime in as needed.	Now it's your turn. Here are three sentences. With your partner, reword these sentences while keeping their meaning intact. I'll circle around and chime in as needed.
WHAT'S NEXT? (1 minute)	*"Today I taught you... While you are working..."*	Today I taught you four new terms. While you are working on your project, do your best to incorporate these terms into your work.	Today I taught you how to make someone else's words your own. While you are working on your project, make sure not to plagiarize, and always document your sources.

FIGURE 4.1 - Project Based Mini-Lessons Adapted from Calkins, 1994

Mini-lessons can take place on a regular basis during project based learning. But, because of the complexities of PBL, we want to avoid getting caught up in always using mini-lessons at the beginning of class or strictly adhering to the five steps. Instead, take what's provided as a starting point, and then use your professional judgment to make it work for your students and your particular context.

During project based learning, briefly bring everyone together daily to check the status of the class before sending students off to work. In other words, instead of always starting class with a mini-lesson or by saying, "It's time to get to work on your projects. Go," you might try succinctly reviewing what they've accomplished and what they still need to do. Then ask, "Does anyone have any glaring questions, thoughts, or concerns before you get started?"

Here, when individuals and groups say they need assistance, you have natural opportunities to address the entire class in a way that benefits everyone. Of course, don't let these discussions carry on for too long, as students need to get to work. If issues require a lengthy response or collaboration, work with individuals and groups, not the entire class.

INTEGRATE EXTENDED LESSONS

Many extended lessons can be the same lessons you normally teach outside of project based learning, as long as they don't last too long. We have found "boring" textbook activities can take on lives of their own when implemented within the context of project based learning. The difference is, because these lessons are used within the context of a project, students can attach their learning to a bigger picture. What they learn becomes that much more meaningful and relevant. As teachers, we can't just assume that our students will make connections between lessons and the project. We must go out of our way to ensure that those connections are explicit when we teach our lessons.

Another option includes project-specific extended lessons. As we'll see in the upcoming examples, these lessons only work when taught within the context of a project based learning experience.

While extended lessons can take on countless shapes and forms, here are eight of our favorites (keeping in mind that some truncated extended lessons can become mini-lessons).

Question brainstorming

Throughout any project, and especially right before students first dive into the work, they will have countless questions swirling around in their heads, including questions about what they're learning and how to execute their projects. Question brainstorming serves as a structured way to get these questions out of students' heads and into the open. First, give students a certain amount of time (about ten minutes) to record any project-related questions. You can do this using a digital tool or a physical space.

As teachers, we had students work in groups, and they wrote their questions on the classroom's back wall, which was covered with a dry-erase board. Then we had a gallery walk so students could see each other's questions. Next, we had a class discussion based on questions and responses. Optionally, prior to class discussion, students could circle their most pertinent questions, which helped to better direct the discussion. Finally, to document the process, we saved all of the brainstormed questions by taking pictures of the back walls and uploading the pictures to the project's digital hub.

We want to make sure the questions and discussion help to inform our students' work (as opposed to the PBL unit following a predetermined path regardless of what takes place). Here are five ways we can make this happen:

- Students sort their most pertinent questions in the order they think they should be answered and then use these questions during their research. Alternatively, students can categorize their questions through such categories as project content, project process, and final product(s). Either way, in the project's interactive directions (detailed in Chapter 6), we can include a section for students to record these questions and the research.

- For the questions that the majority of students have in common, we add them to an anchor chart, which is hung up so everyone can reference them throughout the project. Another option involves using wallspace or a bulletin board and posting the questions by research order or category. During the project, when necessary, more questions can be added.

- If the majority of students have the same question, we plan for at least one proactive mini-lesson or extended lesson that addresses the question. If several students have the same question, it can serve as the basis for a small group conference.

- If the majority of students have the same question, and the question has a direct connection to an academic standard, we can also add the standard's learning target(s) to the project's Progress Assessment Tool. We only recommend altering the Progress Assessment Tool toward the very beginning of a project.

- For a group project, groups can be formed after the question brainstorm based on shared interests uncovered during the process.

Finally, we can allot some time to students discussing and/ or recording their next steps—independently for an individual project, in groups for a group project.

Thinking routines

We were first introduced to thinking routines by the book *Making Thinking Visible* (2011) by Karin Morrison, Ron Ritchhart, and Mark Church. This resource offers twenty-one routines spread out evenly across three categories: introducing and exploring ideas, synthesizing and organizing ideas, and digging deeper into ideas. Question brainstorming, which isn't in the book, serves as an example of a thinking routine.

Thinking routines present students (and adults) with opportunities to learn through thinking, questioning, listening, active sense-making, documenting, and collaboration. Meanwhile, per the book's title, the thinking is made visible, which gives us "not only a window into what students understand but also how they understand it."

Because the same routines can be used repeatedly across different contexts, projects, and subject areas, you might come into a project with students who already understand a specific routine. This saves you from having to repeatedly explain procedures, and allows student learning to remain at the forefront.

Making time for thinking routines sends the message that thinking is a skill that students need to practice and learn, and that it is a critical part of the learning process. When we send these messages, our thinking routines shift from cool activities that exist in isolation to powerful experiences that contribute to creating a culture of thinking, inquiry, and creativity.

Project Zero's Thinking Routine Toolbox can be found at realpbl.com/resources, along with links to websites and organizations that offer additional protocols and resources, such as National School Reform Faculty, School Reform Initiative, and EL Education.

Reading integration

Whether students are reading to learn or learning to read, we can infuse reading into project based learning. One way to do this is to direct students to engage in texts that relate to the project's topic and then encourage them to make connections between the two. The path is simple and straightforward. For example, if the project is about government, students read about government; if the project is about the solar system, students read about the solar system.

Another option is to use texts that connect to what you want students to learn from the project; more specifically, the Umbrella Question, High Impact Takeaways, and learning targets. Here, the texts and the project may or may not share the same topic. As students work through these texts, facilitate focused discussions and activities that deepen their understanding of the project's learning. For teachers, this planning process is more concrete (and easier) if you decide to focus on one project component based on students' needs and/or where you are in the project: the Umbrella Question, one High Impact Takeaway, or one learning target.

To illustrate this second option, let's consider a primary classroom planning a community event. The event itself is the project, and students may also need to learn specific math concepts to help them facilitate the event. The teacher could use picture books to support the teaching and learning of these concepts. These books can be used during read alouds, and students can read them during their independent reading time.

We can bring books and printed publications into our classroom that encompass our projects' topics and/or what we want students to learn from these projects, and we shouldn't have to hesitate to ask our school librarian for help. During a project, we can make its related books and publications more visible and accessible by displaying them in a specific location, such as a designated bookshelf. Students can use these readings for research and can peruse them during free time.

As students conduct research, they may come across texts with which they need help. For texts you deem worthy of tackling, it's an opportunity for you to integrate reading comprehension instruction into project based learning. Instruction can take place during individual and group conferences. When a student finds something significant, we may also use it as the basis for a whole-class lesson.

Writing integration

The same options exist for writing integration: Students can write about the project's topic, or you can create the conditions for students to write in a way that connects to the project's learning. Much like with reading, we can choose one project component based on students' needs and/or where we are in the project. We can ask for students to demonstrate their knowledge, through writing, of this chosen component. For example: "Design a picture book that shows your understanding of the water cycle." Writing genres can vary, and in many instances, we can let students make this choice.

We can also give students prompts and assignments that help them move forward with their projects while deepening their understanding of what they're learning. Here are two options:

- After direct instruction, students write or blog about what they've learned and how it relates to the project's Umbrella Question. When students share their writing with other students through such means as blogging, more learning opportunities are created as students then read and write responses to each other's work through a critical lens.

- Students write responses to any of the reflection questions listed in Chapter 1. If we use prompts that are more open-ended (as opposed to evaluative), we can potentially give students a few questions and then let them decide which one(s) to answer. Throughout a project, students can compile all of their responses in a blog or journal.

To encourage the infusion of PBL content into more open-ended writing experiences, start by simply telling students that this is an option, as the idea most likely won't be on their radar. When you teach writing, model this process for students by incorporating PBL content into your direct instruction; for example, creating and using an exemplar that demonstrates the current lesson's learning goal(s). For instance, many social studies teachers use the *Hamilton* soundtrack to make specific points about history. Lin-Manuel Miranda carefully selected words to not only create a strong beat or harmony, but also to convey a specific story about the past.

Project artifacts and evidence of learning spread throughout the room can also inspire students to blend project based learning with literacy. For example, students' writings on bulletin boards can serve as mentor texts, and anchor charts from Writing Workshop mini-lessons can be referred to by students as they work through their projects.

The PBL Paralysis graphic contains five more ways to support deep literacy integration.

OVERCOMING PBL PARALYSIS
5 WAYS TO SUPPORT DEEP LITERACY INTEGRATION

Include ELA standards in your Progress Assessment Tool. No matter the subject area we teach, we can incorporate ELA standards into our project. Making them part of our Progress Assessment Tool - along with a relevant task(s) in our project's directions - emphasizes their importance while helping to ensure they are taught.

Explicitly teach literacy for your content area. Each content area has a unique style of reading and writing. Teaching students about the typical structure of content-specific text improves comprehension. Understanding the rules and structure of content area writing will help students to produce higher quality work.

Meet students' needs with leveled texts. No matter the grade level we teach, students' reading comprehension skills will vary. By using leveled texts, possibly created using an online tool, we can expose students to approachable material while maintaining our expectations for content understandings.

Collaborate with peers. Before/During project roll-out we can collaborate with literacy teachers at our school. This collaboration can help us to better meet students' needs while also integrating consistent literacy strategies and expectations across all subject areas.

Broaden your definition of literacy. Literacies now include: being intentional with our digital footprint, proper use of hashtags, condensing a powerful message into a few sentences, quality commenting on blog posts, etc. If skills are relevant in the real world, we should be teaching them in our classrooms.

#REALPBL

Demo lessons

These lessons relate to the specific skills or tools students will want or need in order to execute their projects. It's not worth having students uncover this information on their own, either because it's relatively straightforward or because it'll be too much of a struggle. Although we're listing this type of lesson as an extended lesson, these lessons can be as short as a few minutes (showing students how to use a drill) to as long as almost an entire instructional period (walking students through how to use a particular computer program).

In general, we want to try to refrain from fixating on skills and tools for a lengthy amount of time when students have no current use for them. Instead, we immerse students in learning, and when they realize skills and tools are needed to further this learning, we have a plan to provide students with what they need within this authentic context.

Three additional considerations for demo lessons:

- We can always consider chunking a demo lesson, especially if it's going to be long. For example, on day one we can teach students the basics of video editing, and on day two we can explore advanced features and publishing options.

- There will be instances in which all students may not need the demo lesson (e.g., everyone isn't using a drill). But, if we're focusing on a skill or tool all students may need in the long-term, we can still consider conducting the demo for all students. One option is to let students decide whether or not they participate in the lesson.

- If the student expertise exists in our classroom, we can have a student or group of students conduct the demo lesson, possibly with our assistance. Amplifying student experts helps to develop an environment where everyone is seen, both as a teacher and as a learner.

If a demo lesson can be reduced to a series of steps, we can create a visual or video with these steps and distribute it to students when needed, and we can also upload this resource to the project's digital hub so students can access it on their own. Again, students can take the lead in creating and distributing these materials. If applicable, the same materials (teacher and/or student created) can be uploaded and used year after year, helping to grow an expansive library of options from which students can choose.

Finally, if a demo lesson's steps are concrete and easy to follow, we may forego the lesson altogether and simply make the visual or video accessible to students.

Presentation skills

If you plan to formally assess or possibly grade students on their presentation, you need to teach this skill. Even if students won't be formally assessed or graded, it's a valuable skill worth teaching, especially since it's involved in the majority of project based learning experiences. In the Introduction, the *Job Outlook 2020* survey lists "communication skills (verbal)" as the seventh most sought-after attribute in prospective employees.

While the components of an effective presentation vary by grade level, some consistent areas of focus include:

- Clarity and organization
- Posture
- Eye contact
- Tone

- Volume
- Supporting materials
- Audience responsiveness
- Collaboration (if applicable)

Toward the beginning of your students' first project based learning experience, we recommend reviewing with students the components of an effective presentation. Additionally, expose students to exemplars, such as TED Talks, which they can evaluate based on these components.

You might also give these components to students and then work with them to define the success criteria for each one, with help from exemplars. This process is the equivalent of students contributing to the creation of their Progress Assessment Tool. In this case, your finished document, which you can use to assess presentation skills, would have presentation components in the left column (instead of learning targets), success criteria in the middle column, and feedback in the right column. Optionally, you can rewrite each component as a statement or question. For example: "I can maintain a consistent, professional tone" or "Can I maintain a consistent, professional tone?"

For each project in which students will be presenting, set aside time for them to practice, while they keep in mind who their audience will be during their eventual presentation. As public speaking expert Michael Port tells us in *Steal the Show* (2015), "The simplest way to overcome stage fright or performance anxiety is to actually know what you're doing when you're on stage or in a high-pressure situation." Port also emphasizes the idea that most of us don't actually know *how* to practice. If your students already have a Progress Assessment Tool and are familiar with it, it can be used for guidance as they craft, practice, and give their presentations, and then used as the basis for teacher, peer, and self-assessment during practice rounds. Proactively and reactively, we can also teach lessons that connect to our presentation components.

If you're looking for resources specific to slide design, we recommend *Presentation Zen* by Garr Reynolds and pretty much anything by Nancy Duarte, including *slide:ology* and *Resonate*.

Outside experts

Outside experts can help give a project an authentic feel while also enhancing student learning. As classroom teachers, we brought in experts to work alongside students and to present to students, and they were in the audience when students presented their projects. In some instances, these experts were parents or guardians of students, so it is worth finding out what everyone does for a living. An optional survey can help, as long as we make our intentions known. Other accessible connections can include family members of students from classrooms other than our own, teachers and staff in our school or district, community members, and any other friends or colleagues.

If our students are capable, we can encourage them to arrange for expert visits, possibly with our assistance. As classroom teachers, we typically worked with students to email our experts. Now, we regularly use social media to make these same connections. Countless experts are more easily accessible via social media, and many of them are more than willing to work with students. Prior to any expert's visit, we (or our students) tell them about the current project and what we hope to get out of the visit. If necessary, we work with the expert to plan for what will take place.

Outside experts can be difficult to schedule. If you add them to your calendar for a specific day or week based on where you think you'll be in the project, there's always the chance the project won't go as planned, and you won't need the experts for the specified date or time. The best advice we have is to be flexible and hope the experts are as well, or use asynchronous tools (e.g., Google Docs and discussion forums) so experts can contribute when it's convenient for them. Remote visits (e.g., Zoom and Google Meet) are also an option.

If experts will be in the audience when students present, inform students at the outset of the project. This expert participation will serve as motivation and influence students as they execute their projects and plan their presentations with a specific audience in mind. You can also put structures in place for experts, and possibly everyone else in the audience, to provide feedback to the presenters.

Research

When we first think of research, what usually comes to mind is the traditional research paper. This involved photocopying pages from books and printing out articles. From the pages and printouts, students might highlight passages and use them to develop their own ideas. Once it's their own, they regurgitate it in another format, such as a research paper, poster, or slides. While research still should include books and articles, it can also involve our outside experts, interviews, fieldwork, experiments, prototyping, YouTube, videos, photographs, songs, and more.

If we want students to conduct research effectively, we need to teach them how to do it. Research involves, but isn't limited to, these ten phases. We won't call them "steps" because 1) depending on the situation, not all phases may apply, 2) nothing ever happens in a linear fashion, and 3) students will navigate the phases based on how their research unfolds. For example, more questions will likely surface (phase 1) as students make connections between multiple pieces of content (phase 5). Therefore, these additional questions may call for students to "go back" a few phases.

- Knowing what questions to ask and what information to look for
- Finding content
- Differentiating between credible sources and those that are unreliable
- Consuming content (e.g., reading, watching, listening)
- Making connections between the multiple pieces of content
- Extracting relevant information and organizing it according to the connections
- Combining relevant information from the multiple pieces of content
- Making the relevant information their own by rewording, adding their voice, and refining
- Publishing or presenting their work and what they've learned
- Citing sources

By identifying phases, we're also identifying teaching points for when you teach students how to research. Then you can more easily pinpoint where you can provide more or less support based on your students' capabilities. For example, if we consider finding resources for older students, direct instruction could involve brief demos of a library database and a search engine. For younger students, you may all but remove this phase by proactively providing them with a list of resources from which they can choose.

Finally, you can call upon the school librarian or another expert to help with research. But research skills aren't just for the library.

Students should be developing and using these skills within the context of their work, as often as possible.

Ross: As an elementary school principal, I had the privilege of working with a multi-talented librarian, Lisa Straubinger, and we reconfigured her schedule to include two forty-five-minute flex periods a day. During this time, she was able to push into classrooms to blur the line between "class time" and "library time."

FINAL THOUGHTS

In *Focus* (2011), Mike Schmoker tells a story that represents what he sees in schools.

> He [a highly respected teacher] is always innovating. He has initiated interdisciplinary teaching, heavy use of technology, hands-on activities, and lots of "project based learning." His students do very little reading and even less writing. But they spend lots of time going to and from the library, often preparing, making, and then listening (listlessly) to each other's flashy but unfocused PowerPoint presentations. And like the majority of the teachers at his school, he doesn't even realize that his lessons and projects are devoid of modeling, guided practice, or checks for understanding. Nonetheless, the teacher is highly regarded for his emphasis on "active" learning, on "integrating technology" into his "project-based" assignments. Why? *Because instead of coherent curriculum and effective lessons, these are the school's operative priorities; they are the focus of praise and professional development in his school and district.*

When we originally read this paragraph, it truly resonated with us, as early on in our teaching careers, we easily could have been this teacher. We suspect that this paragraph resonates with many of you, as well; either you see yourself in these words, or they remind you of a certain colleague or two.

In this respect, we've learned lessons as we've progressed through our careers.

First: Let's stop wearing "progressive" as a badge of honor. Our classrooms aren't about us; they're about our students. Flash without substance means students' needs aren't being met. This is our top priority.

Second: When we infuse direct instruction into project based learning, our flash (progressive practice) becomes the substance, as this combination helps to create the optimal conditions for student learning.

In the end, if we're comfortable with who we were a few years ago, there's a problem. So, even though we went through our stage of "direct instruction disdain," we needed to endure that to get to where we are now. And, in a few more years, we know we'll look back at our current work and tell ourselves we can do better.

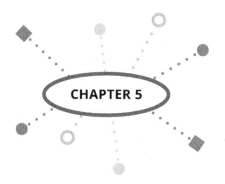

CHAPTER 5

REAL QUESTION:

How Do I Build a PBL Culture?

You can borrow or steal a technique, but
never a philosophy or culture.
— MICHAEL FULLAN, AUTHOR OF *THE SIX SECRETS OF CHANGE*

ROSS: TOWARD THE start of my project based learning journey, I found myself a few weeks into the new school year ... and it was starting to go downhill.

Even though I believed I had all the answers, students didn't seem to be buying into my approach, and several families were confused as to what was going on in the classroom. To make matters worse, one of my students disenrolled, leaving for a private school in the area. While I wasn't entirely responsible for this move, the parent of another student informed me that my radical teaching style was the deciding factor. And, during this same conversation, she tried to tell me about concerns from other parents.

Her words fell on deaf ears (and she knew it) because I thought I knew best.

Soon after this conversation, the situation came to a head during Meet the Teacher Night. A few parents, who obviously didn't feel that they were being heard, went out of their way to embarrass me and mock my teaching style in front of the other parents. The whole time, I was literally counting down the minutes until the session would end, while using all of my patience to keep my composure and respond to each accusation in the most politically correct way possible.

While most of what happened next is now a blur, I do remember everyone leaving the classroom, and then I sat down at my desk for quite a while in an attempt to mentally process what had just happened and pull myself back together. During this time, one of the parents stopped by again to touch base and console me a bit. Then my principal, Dr. Anthony Moyer, paid me a visit to see how everything went. Not holding anything back, I explained to Tony in detail what had transpired (which speaks to the kind of relationship we had).

At the end of the night, I checked my mailbox and found that Tony had taped the following quote to it:

> It is not the critic who counts; not the man who points out how the strong man stumbles, or where the doer of deeds could have done them better. The credit belongs to the man who is actually in the arena, whose face is marred by dust and sweat and blood; who strives valiantly; who errs, who comes short again and again, because there is no effort without error and shortcoming; but who does actually strive to do the deeds; who knows great enthusiasms, the great devotions; who spends himself in a worthy cause; who at the best knows in the end the triumph of high achievement, and who at the worst, if he fails, at least fails while daring greatly, so that his place shall never be with those cold and timid souls who neither know victory nor defeat.

This Theodore Roosevelt quote is from his highly regarded 1910 speech, "Citizenship in a Republic," also now known as "The Man in the Arena." The quote and speech were made even more popular when Brené Brown featured them in her now bestselling book, *Daring Greatly*.

I took the quote with me into the adjacent conference room, had a seat, and cried for what had to be about a good ten minutes. All of the night's twists and turns had gotten to me, and I just had to let it all out.

Looking back, I realize that one problem was my arrogance. Another issue, which we'll address in this chapter, is that implementing best practice overnight is not best practice, because people—students and their parents or guardians—are impacted by every decision we make.

Rather than railroading our ideas through while attempting to sell others on what we think is best, we can take a collaborative approach, meeting others where they are and moving along until our practices are where we think they should be. And, at the end of every school year, we'll most likely have to painstakingly press the reset button.

REAL ANSWERS:

LEARN FROM COMMON MISTAKES

We believe that project based learning is a harmonious compilation of best practices joined together. While the practices are not new, the approach in its entirety can represent a shift in mindset from a culture centered on control and compliance to a culture centered on students, inquiry, and creativity.

Unfortunately, many of the practices and policies present in our schools serve as barriers to this type of thinking. We have collaborated with countless schools and districts in efforts to move toward learner-centered experiences. Often, we're tempted to begin these shifts with a direct focus on the instructional moves employed by the teacher. Certainly, this makes sense; the teacher is the individual with the most control over a learner's day-to-day experiences. But as management guru Peter Drucker famously wrote, "Culture eats strategy for breakfast," we must think bigger; we must think *beyond* instruction.

When setting the stage for project based learning, we regularly witness two common mistakes.

The first is not setting the stage at all. (*Ross:* This is the mistake I made.) This approach can work if a culture of inquiry and creativity already exists and maybe if students are already learning through learner-centered experiences like project based learning, design thinking, Genius Hour, and makerspaces. But, more often than not, this mistake involves, without forewarning, taking project based learning and sticking it right in the middle of what most would call a traditional classroom environment.

In other words, we're attempting to retrofit culture, as opposed to changing the system altogether. And then, when this approach doesn't work, we sometimes get an "I told you so," and many revert back to what they were doing before the attempt. In short, we've wasted time, we now have more skeptics than before (or upset parents at Meet the Teacher Night), and students have missed out on valuable opportunities.

The second mistake is believing that culture and project based learning transpire sequentially. We spend a few weeks building our PBL culture, most likely toward the beginning of the school year. Then, once we believe we're good to go, we unleash our projects throughout the remainder of the year, never again intentionally working on culture, or failing to realize that everything we do

134

influences culture in one way or another. In other words, when it comes to culture, we set it and forget it. In reality, per John Kotter in *Leading Change* (2012), "Cultural change comes at the end of a transformation, not the beginning." So, while we should absolutely lay the foundation before we ask our students to dive into project based learning, we must then spend the entire year building on top of this foundation through the interactions, relationships, and learning experiences we promote.

Now that we know the mistakes you have to watch out for, let's explore how to build a PBL culture. More specifically, we'll look at establishing relationships with students, explicitly teaching students how to collaborate, and laying the foundation.

ESTABLISH RELATIONSHIPS

Erin: During the first week of a school year, I was standing in the hallway of one of the middle schools in my district. A teacher walked by a student and greeted the student by name. The student smiled broadly and said, "Good morning!" Then the student turned to another and said, "This place is so big, but so many people know our names already."

Every moment counts.

For many educators, our interactions with students are second nature. We ask about their weekends and worry about them when they look more tired than usual. Educators, however, are humans, too. We also fall victim to the daily grind and the endless pressures. When something has to give, oftentimes it is the time we invest in knowing our students. Teachers may see 150 or more students each day, but students have ten or fewer teachers. If a student goes through an entire day and no one says her name or asks how she's doing, are we setting her up for success?

Truthfully, if we don't prioritize relationships, nothing else matters. And, nothing else from this book will work, at least not as well as you want. As Rita Pierson announced during her TED Talk, "Every Kid Needs a Champion" (2013):

> Kids don't learn from people they don't like ... Every child deserves a champion, an adult who will never give up on them, who understands the power of connection, and insists that they become the best that they can possibly be.

With all of this in mind, here are four ways to establish relationships with students, with your PBL culture in mind. We caution against turning these strategies into a series of events, though; relationships should be woven into the fabric of what you do on an ongoing and never-ending basis.

Be present for students

Consider these two scenarios from a student's point of view.

Scenario 1. You enter the room unnoticed and scan the space with your eyes. First, you see the person who posted something unkind on your social media feed last night. Then you see the person who almost knocked you over in the hallway, leaving you unsure whether or not it was purposeful. Your teacher is behind the desk, possibly checking email or preparing to take attendance. You notice the board, and the assignments for the day increase your feeling of dread.

Scenario 2. You enter the room and are greeted by your teacher, who is standing by the door. "Good morning, Matthew! How was your art show last night?" You respond to your teacher's question. The teacher, who seems to understand your stress level, mentions as you take your seat, "There is a lot on the agenda today, but we are going to walk through it all together." You are still aware of the other stressors in the room, but they are no longer center stage in the narrative.

For students of all ages, the mere presence of an adult improves their perception of physical and psychological safety. The teacher in the second scenario created an immediate connection with the student as he walked into the room. This connection added to his feeling of safety, while demonstrating that he was known and valued. When you actively engage with the classroom, you can keep a finger on the pulse of the room, promote positive energy, and establish a rapport with students. Meanwhile, the teacher behind the desk in the first scenario was seemingly unaware of the inner workings of the classroom dynamic, and might increase a student's sense of frustration and isolation without even knowing it.

> WHEN WE SAY, "THE KIDS I HAVE COULDN'T DO THIS!" ARE WE TALKING ABOUT OUR STUDENTS' LIMITATIONS OR OUR OWN?

Children struggle with fitting in, have disagreements with their families, and say mean things to each other on social media. As educators, we cannot make all of the trials and tribulations of our students disappear. But, if we decide to ignore these problems because it's not in our job description, we're missing out on our greatest opportunities to make a difference. Most students (and adults) want us to send a message: "I see you. I get you." When a trusted adult acknowledges students, addresses them by name, and demonstrates an interest in their well-being, students are far more likely to be successful, in and out of school.

Never underestimate students

When we started out with project based learning, we enjoyed showing off our projects and students' work to other teachers (maybe a little too much). On several occasions, teachers responded to our projects by saying our approach was developmentally inappropriate.

Teachers also sometimes reacted to our projects with, "The kids I have couldn't do this!"

For a few years, we thought our students were uniquely talented and that other teachers were working with students who were somehow less capable. In time, we started asking ourselves a question that we believe we should all be asking: When we say, "The kids I have couldn't do this!" are we talking about our students' limitations or our own?

Often, students are limited by our own comfort zones, and we're experiencing an expectations gap rather than an achievement gap. We have found that when we set the bar high, show confidence in our students, and act like they should be able to meet our expectations, not only do they usually hit the bar, they typically jump over it! In the words of an anonymous six-year-old, "My teacher thought I was smarter than I was—so I was!" When we act this way, we foster growth mindsets (more on this idea later in this chapter), while also promoting what psychologist Albert Bandura (1997) calls self-efficacy: "An individual's belief in his or her capacity to execute behaviors necessary to produce specific performance attainments."

For students, this is the belief that *they* are responsible for their own success, not their teachers, families, or peers. Students with high self-efficacy are more likely to embrace challenging tasks, while viewing failures as learning opportunities.

In addition, we have seen children as young as kindergarten set goals and reflect on their progress, conduct research with scaffolded materials, publish their work for an authentic audience, engage with community members, plan a schoolwide community tea party, and put on a production of their favorite book. We enjoy watching primary teachers raise the bar, as their students' accomplishments help to refute the argument that students from younger grade levels are too young to "learn this way."

Prioritize students, not curriculum

Ross: A few years into teaching, I asked my students to design one of the last days of school, and a handful of students decided to put on a talent show. I was completely surprised when one of them, Gabbie, beautifully sang a few songs for the rest of the class (complete with background music). I was blown away by her performance, but also ashamed that the entire school year had gone by and I hadn't found out about my students' talents. I promised myself that I wouldn't make that mistake again.

A few years later, I discovered that one of my students, Shayna, was struggling to adjust to my fourth grade classroom. I scheduled a meeting with her parents, where they told me that Shayna felt the class was moving too fast and she didn't have the time and space to express herself. During this same meeting, I also learned that she could play guitar and was a huge Beatles fan, and that her favorite song was "She Came in Through the Bathroom Window." In order to tap into her passions and help her connect with the class, I asked Shayna to bring her guitar to school to play a few songs for her peers. This "concert" was the beginning of her year turning around for the better.

Toward the very end of *Hacking Project Based Learning*, we cite an anonymous quote that says, "Some teachers taught the curriculum today. Other teachers taught students today. And there's a big difference." In both of my examples, this was the problem: I prioritized what I thought I had to get through, not what was relevant to my students.

If we want to build relationships and make our classrooms more about our students (not us), we can't fake student voice and choice. We can't have our projects, activities, and lessons set in stone before the school year even begins. We can get better at listening to our students and being responsive to what makes each one of them unique.

Match words with actions

In *The First 90 Days* (2013), Michael Watkins tells us, "Finally, and above all, take care to live the vision you articulate. A vision that is undercut by inconsistent leadership behaviors ... is worse than no vision at all. Be sure you are prepared to walk the talk."

Connections can be made between this quote and some of education's conflicting messages, several of which Katie Martin points out in *Learner-Centered Innovation* (2018). Here are three of them: Students are provided with their own laptops, but cell phones are banned; we believe no two students are alike, but standardized assessment practices are used to measure performance and success; and we believe that when students share their learning, they experience more meaningful education experiences, but all grades are based on assignments turned in to the teacher.

As classroom teachers, we might not be able to control some conflicting messages. And due to school and district policies, we may have to teach in ways we don't believe are best for students. (But even then, we have a right to respectfully seek clarification from administrators.) Within our space, we can still work to make sure our actions match our words. For example:

- When we ask students to take risks, we encourage and support them when they make mistakes.

- When we get students excited about owning their learning, we embed voice and choice into our projects.

- When we tell students they'll have our support, we constantly meet with them as they do the work.

- When we want the emphasis to be on learning (not compliance), we move students forward with feedback (not grades).

- When we put students in groups and ask them to collaborate, we proactively and reactively teach them how to do so.

To help ensure that our actions are consistent with our words and the classroom vision we articulate, we can only promise what we can deliver, continually reflect on our practices, and ask for and consider feedback from colleagues and students.

When our words and actions are aligned, we build trust with students. This trust, which can be difficult to build and easy to lose, allows students to feel safe. And when students (and adults) feel safe, we've created the conditions for them to enjoy and embrace their learning while also helping them maximize their potential.

TEACH COLLABORATION

Student collaboration is a cornerstone of any thriving classroom culture, but collaboration can break down when students have differing ideas or opinions. At that point, students typically decide to divide and conquer. But collaboration is not defined by slicing up a workload and then smashing independent pieces into a final product. Collaboration, not to be confused with group work, is an interdependent give-and-take, where the collective progress of the group improves the overall body of work.

As mentioned in the Introduction, the *Job Outlook 2020* survey lists "ability to work in a team" as the second most sought-after attribute in prospective employees. This is a skill we need to teach our students, both proactively (before projects, and before disagreements occur among students) and reactively (during projects, when issues arise). However, we often miss that mark.

Here were two of our initial approaches to teaching collaboration during project based learning:

1. All of our rubrics had a graded component for collaboration, which read, "I was the best teammate that I could be, and I continuously contributed to the project throughout its creation!"

2. We put students in groups, told them to get along, and got upset with them when there were issues.

In other words, we didn't actually *teach* collaboration. And, "Simply putting kids around a table and telling them to work together does not teach them collaboration skills" (Quinn, 2012).

For a few years, we never actually taught students how to collaborate, yet we assessed them on this skill. We expected them to excel at it even though many adults around them struggled with it. Telling students we will evaluate something doesn't mean they will automatically adapt to meet expectations. While we can debate whether or not collaboration should be graded, if we are going to grade or formally assess it, we need to make sure it has been taught.

The PBL Paralysis graphic details a process for how you can teach collaboration.

OVERCOMING PBL PARALYSIS
6 STEPS TO STUDENTS UNCOVERING COLLABORATION

One approach is to simply tell students the features of effective collaboration and then make sure these features are followed. A better approach, to promote student ownership and deeper understanding, is to have students uncover these features. Here's a process to consider:

1. The teacher poses the question: What is collaboration?

2. Students are exposed to various collaboration exemplars through classroom observations (in person and in video) and by reading articles on the topic, which don't necessarily have to be school related.

3. In groups, students are asked to consider these exemplars and their experiences in order to list the features of effective collaboration - while also considering what collaboration should look, sound, and feel like.

4. Everyone comes together as a class to share their features. A definitive class list is created by eliminating duplicates, combining similar features, and by including those that are most relevant.

5. The definitive class list is added to an anchor chart, which is hung up so it can be referenced and reinforced throughout the year.

6. Throughout the year, the list is revised as necessary.

Each item on the definitive class list can serve as a teaching point and the basis for a lesson on collaboration, which is far less overwhelming than attempting to teach collaboration all at once, in its entirety.

Here are the components of collaboration according to PBLWorks:

- Takes responsibility
- Helps the team
- Respects others
- Makes and follows agreements
- Organizes work
- Works as a whole team

Optionally, you can use these collaboration components as the basis for a Progress Assessment Tool that you distribute or create with students, and you can facilitate lessons that involve the components and their success criteria. During and after projects, use the document for teacher, peer, and self-assessment. Alternatively, make a Progress Assessment Tool out of the definitive class list generated by the activity in the graphic.

A unique approach, more suitable for older students, is to expose students to Patrick Lencioni's five dysfunctions of a team: absence of trust, fear of conflict, lack of commitment, avoidance of accountability, and inattention to results. For students (and adults), knowledge of these dysfunctions promotes self-awareness that helps them proactively avoid pitfalls while also being cognizant of problems that may emerge. Much like the collaboration components, you can give students these dysfunctions and then work with them to determine what it looks like when each one exists. Only in this case, rather than using the term "success criteria," you might name it something like "dysfunction criteria." Also, you can use Lencioni's book (or excerpts), *The Five Dysfunctions of a Team*, to facilitate lessons on the topic.

You can also scaffold collaboration for students by providing them with sentence stems. Compile these stems on a handout for students, or add the stems to an anchor chart. Either way, these stems are scaffolds, and the eventual goal is for students to collaborate without the visual support.

Here are a few examples of what these stems could look like:

- What I hear you saying is ...
- I agree with you because ...
- Adding to what [insert name] said ...
- I understand what you mean, *and* ...
- Based on my experience ...
- Please say more about ...
- What makes you say that?

Lastly, for students to collaborate, model the way by seeking first to understand. While engaged with coworkers, colleagues, and friends, consciously work at having and showing interest in their thoughts, ideas, and experiences. This can be easier said than done, of course. According to Stephen Covey in *The 7 Habits of Highly Effective People* (2004), "Most people do not listen with the intent to understand; they listen with the intent to reply. They're either speaking or preparing to speak. They're filtering everything through their own paradigms, reading their autobiography into other people's lives." Nonetheless, if it's what you're asking of your students, you should be doing it as well.

LAY A FOUNDATION

As previously mentioned, culture and project based learning don't transpire sequentially, and culture isn't something we just set and forget. When building a PBL culture, you have to start somewhere, and there's no better time to lay your foundation than the beginning of the school year. Or, if you want to kick off project based learning later in the year, add restraint by first preparing your students for what they're about to experience.

Here are four ways we initiated a PBL culture with our students.

Marshmallow Challenge

Hands-on challenges, such as the Marshmallow Challenge, can set the tone for project based learning. Give groups of four to five students the following materials: twenty sticks of spaghetti, one yard of masking tape, one yard of string, one marshmallow, and one pair of scissors. Then give them twenty minutes to build the tallest freestanding structure possible, with their entire marshmallow at the top. The winning team was the one that had the tallest structure measured from the table's surface to the top of the marshmallow.

After the challenge, start building students' habit of critical reflection by asking them to discuss the following questions in their groups. Once they have their answers, bring them together for class discussion:

- If you had all the time in the world to complete the Marshmallow Challenge, what would you do differently?

- If you could go back in time and talk to yourself before you completed the Marshmallow Challenge, what is one piece of advice you would offer?

- What is one mistake that you and your group made while doing the Marshmallow Challenge? How did you fix it?

- What school subject is the Marshmallow Challenge? Is it more than one? Explain.

- Why do you think we are starting the year with the Marshmallow Challenge?

Next, we watched the TED Talk based on the Marshmallow Challenge, "Build a Tower, Build a Team" (2010) by Tom Wujec. One key takeaway was that kindergartners were able to outperform business students. While business students "are trained to find the single right plan," kindergartners keep building successive prototypes "so they have multiple times to fix [their tower] along the way. ... With each version, kids get instant feedback about what works and what doesn't work." This exemplifies the iterative process, an idea we talked about as a class.

If you don't like the Marshmallow Challenge (or you've already done it with your students), use any other activity as long as students are engaging in critical thinking, collaboration, reflection, and possibly more. For example, *Creative Confidence* by Tom Kelley and David Kelley contains ten creative challenges that can help students (and adults) unleash their inner creativity. These challenges are also in the article, "10 Exercises to Build Your Creative Confidence," found at realpbl.com/resources.

Exposure to inquiry-rich companies

We frequently exposed our students to readings, videos, and TED Talks that influenced our teaching and, consequently, our classroom culture. For example, during the first week of school, we watched a Travel Channel segment that featured the working conditions of the Googleplex (Google headquarters) in Mountain View, California. These conditions included such luxuries as gourmet cafeteria food, multiple state-of-the-art fitness centers, sleeping pods, on-site laundry and dry cleaning, and free rental cars. Afterward, we read an article on Google's culture. Then we asked the question: How can we make our classroom like Google?

As a class, we discussed which components of the company's culture we could make our own (and how), and what we could do to ensure a successful year.

Here are fifteen additional resources we have used while exploring classroom culture to develop the skills and dispositions endorsed by many of these authors. Some of these resources also have strong ties to inquiry-rich companies.

Books (or excerpts)

- *Creative Confidence* by Tom Kelley and David Kelley (IDEO)
- *Creativity, Inc.* by Ed Catmull (Pixar)
- *Change by Design* by Tim Brown (IDEO)
- *Radical Candor* by Kim Scott
- *Steal Like an Artist* by Austin Kleon

Videos

- IDEO on *60 Minutes* (design thinking)
- *Caine's Arcade* (Genius Hour)
- Austin's Butterfly featuring Ron Berger (critique, feedback, and the iterative process)
- A Day in the Life of an Amazon Package
- Apple media events (We watched product releases to study presentation techniques and slide design.)

TED Talks

- "Do Schools Kill Creativity?" by Sir Ken Robinson
- "How to Manage for Collective Creativity" by Linda Hill

- "Stop Stealing Dreams" by Seth Godin
- "Math Class Needs a Makeover" by Dan Meyer
- "Every Kid Needs a Champion" by Rita Pierson

During every year's Meet the Teacher Night, we also recommended to families a few resources (two to three books and two to three videos) that inspired our teaching and would inform their children's experiences in our classrooms.

Growth mindset versus fixed mindset

These terms, coined by researcher and professor Carol Dweck (2016), contrast those who view intelligence and personality as traits we can develop, as opposed to traits that are innate and unchangeable. The following descriptions are from her book *Mindset.*

More specifically, regarding a growth mindset:

> *Growth mindset* is based on the belief that your basic qualities are things you can cultivate through your efforts, your strategies, and help from others. Although people may differ in every which way—in their initial talents and aptitudes, interests, or temperaments—everyone can change and grow through application and experience.

Regarding a fixed mindset:

> Believing that your qualities are carved in stone—the *fixed mindset*—creates an urgency to prove yourself over and over. If you have only a certain amount of intelligence, a certain personality, and a certain moral character—well, then you'd better prove that you have a healthy dose of them.

Both mindsets exist along a continuum because we're not entirely one or the other. Understanding mindsets is critical for learners of all ages. Our mindset influences how we view ourselves, how we handle feedback, the extent to which we're willing to take creative risks, our relationships with others, and, ultimately, how we lead our lives.

As a class, we viewed video clips of Dweck and her colleagues, read articles, and explored parts of her book *Mindset*. Through this work, we learned about the two mindsets with an emphasis on recognizing and fostering a growth mindset. Students then wrote a few paragraphs or recorded videos explaining how having a growth mindset could help them during the school year and beyond.

Countless classrooms, schools, and districts have explored the two types of mindsets, and it's easy to find resources such as posters and bulletin boards. However, we find it most beneficial to create these displays with our students based on the information they uncover during their own learning. These displays can serve as reminders of the value of having a growth mindset and can support students in shifting their mindset. Also, we can formally revisit this topic toward the end of the school year, giving students time to reflect upon how their mindset may have changed since the first day of school.

Communication with families

One question we used to get from families was, "What's going to happen next year [when next year's teacher doesn't teach like you do]?" In fact, since becoming administrators, more progressive teachers often tell us they're dealing with this same question or problem. Our response to this question has been and always will be the same: We do the best we can with our students while they're with us; we shouldn't give them less of an experience simply because next year will be different.

That being said, with every school year that went by, we got more and more progressive with our teaching, which also meant our styles became increasingly further removed from what our students' families had come to expect from their children's education. So, every year we tried to be proactive and intentional about overcommunicating with parents and guardians, while making it known what students and their families would experience throughout the year.

Here are a few ways we communicated:

- In our opening letter to families, we offered to meet with parents or guardians before the start of the school year. To be as accessible as possible, the letter also contained our cell phone numbers. Of course, we realize that not all teachers are comfortable giving out this information, but we can say it never led to any problems.

- About a month into the school year, we hosted a parent information night with a focus on project based learning and the different technologies we'd be using throughout the year. These technologies included our classroom website, our learning management system (e.g., Canvas, Schoology, Google Classroom), and Google Workspace for Education Fundamentals. The presentation emphasized how families could use these tools to stay informed as to what was happening at school.

- We used a school-friendly text messaging service, Remind, to send families text message updates about once a week.

You might also consider using social media to communicate with your families, as most of them are already on social media, so it doesn't come across as "one more thing." Use platforms based on what families are already using. We've used Instagram, Facebook, and Twitter to interact with our stakeholders, and public response is always resoundingly positive.

Finally, even with all of these technologies at our disposal, face-to-face communication, video conferences, and phone calls should be our defaults in order to be as personable as possible.

FINAL THOUGHTS

Culture doesn't exist in isolation, and every decision we make impacts the culture of our space. This entire book is full of practices we can leverage to build, maintain, and grow a PBL culture. Some of these practices include: promote relevance, not just engagement (Introduction); don't grade projects (Chapters 1 and 2); collaborate with students to design flexible learning spaces (Chapter 6); and let students publish their work for an audience larger than just the teacher (Chapters 1 and 8).

Erin: Since high school, I have been involved in teaching others how to swim. As a general practice, beginning swimmers start their lessons on the stairs of the pool. They use their hands to splash water on their shoulders and face, and then they carefully wiggle their bodies along the side of the pool while still gripping the edge to practice kicking their feet. A few brave individuals may try placing their face in the water. This deliberate process takes time, but the intentional steps allow for individuals to acclimate themselves to the water and pool.

Swim instructors use their knowledge of the water and the typical insecurities of beginning swimmers to manipulate the environment, which helps learners comfortably shift their focus to their swimming skills. The same is true for our classrooms: taking the time to intentionally prepare our students for upcoming experiences helps them focus on the learning.

Meanwhile, when advanced swimmers enter the pool, they may be comfortable enough with the water to dive right in. But, like any athlete, they spend time allowing their bodies to adjust to the water. Similarly, older students need time to adjust to a new context. Although some may have previous experience with project based learning, they will require time to learn classroom expectations and connect with the teacher and other learners. Ultimately, regardless of age or experience, our learners benefit from a learning environment designed with intentionality.

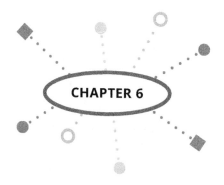

CHAPTER 6

REAL QUESTION:

How Do I Manage the Chaos?

An effective teacher manages a classroom. An ineffective teacher disciplines a classroom.
— HARRY WONG AND ROSEMARY T. WONG,
AUTHORS OF *THE FIRST DAYS OF SCHOOL*

A FEW YEARS AGO, we had the opportunity to keynote the Los Angeles Unified School District's gifted symposium. The theme of the conference was Chaos Coordinators. (It was awesome; there were shirts and everything.) While catchy and engaging, we felt the theme itself revealed an often-dismissed truth about our work: When we shift from teacher-centered to learner-centered classrooms, the assumption is that chaos will ensue.

A kernel of truth exists in this idea of chaos. During presentations, we usually ask participants to discuss the differences between projects and project based learning. Without fail, someone always describes project based learning as chaos. And we won't lie to you; project based learning is not neat and tidy. For this reason, we cannot rush or overlook the steps we take to prepare our students for project based learning, especially since many of them have grown accustomed to playing the game of school. As we touched on in the previous chapter, learners need to feel safe if we want them to push beyond their comfort zones. In addition to developing interpersonal relationships, students' perception of safety is also impacted by the way we structure our learning space and our learning experiences.

Practitioners want to know how to proactively avoid and manage this potential chaos. We address this predicament across several responses that, when handled with intentionality, can help to support a smoother PBL process.

REAL ANSWERS:

ESTABLISH CLASSROOM ROUTINES

Erin: Even though I was trained in project based instructional methods in college and spent my years as a classroom teacher implementing and revising PBL units, I believe I learned the most about managing a working classroom while serving as a middle school assistant principal.

Related arts teachers in classes such as family consumer science, art, tech ed, and physical education engage students in performance tasks and projects throughout the majority of their class periods. By nature, these courses are project based and the instructors become masterful at managing the learning environment. In particular, they work to ensure their classroom routines are flawless.

If you were to observe Mrs. Kukitz's seventh grade art class, for example, you would see students enter the room and immediately begin to gather their materials. After gathering the items they need for the work period, students get started on their assignments while the teacher takes attendance and checks in with individuals. Once everyone is settled, Mrs. Kukitz may invite the students to join her at one of the tables for a demonstration. All of the students get up, push in their stools, leave their materials at their seats, and gather around the display table in a semicircle.

> EDUCATORS SHOULDN'T BE DESIGNING LEARNING SPACES FOR PINTEREST; STUDENTS SHOULD BE DESIGNING LEARNING SPACES FOR THEMSELVES.

These smooth transitions are no accident. Mrs. Kukitz starts each year by explicitly modeling and developing the routines necessary for student success. To generate buy-in for the desired behaviors, she uses the exciting aspects of her course, such as using a hot glue gun for the first time.

In many related arts courses, teachers use clear guidelines and routines to ensure physical safety. You can use a similar process in any classroom to keep things running smoothly.

Here are three steps to implementing classroom routines:

1. **Establish urgency:** There is a difference between a routine and a rule. While rules are often broad and widely applicable, a routine has a clear purpose and fulfills a particular need. Start by brainstorming with students to determine which needs require a routine (e.g., collecting materials, borrowing a book, visiting the art room), and then work with the group to establish clear action steps.

2. **Model success:** It's important that students understand what a successful routine looks like in action. Walk students through the process, discussing

possible pitfalls along the way, and then ask them to brainstorm how they will know if the routine is successful. Discuss what happens when the routine does not occur successfully, and use that as an opportunity to uncover natural consequences. ("If your project is not returned to the correct spot, it may be lost.")

3. **Follow up:** We know working with students means that every day is an adventure, and a routine you put in place might get a little rocky. If the routine requires revision, don't hesitate to discuss that with students. Often, they will just need a reminder. If so, revisit Step 2 and model it again. Learners of all ages benefit from revisiting expectations.

So much of what happens in our daily lives at school is spontaneous: misbehaving technology, fire drills, disruptive behavior, and more. Routines add predictability to the day, which can help students feel more comfortable. Constructing meaningful routines with our students is crucial if you want to maintain sanity in a project based class.

DESIGN FLEXIBLE LEARNING SPACES

Flexible learning spaces are a trendy topic in education. Just like any instructional shift, they should be approached with caution. Our spaces, when designed with intentionality, should support and elevate project based learning (and pretty much all other teaching and learning), while also helping to strengthen culture. But if we have the money, it's also easy to fake change by buying a whole bunch of stuff without putting in the actual work to shift our practices.

According to Scott Doorley and Scott Witthoft (2012), "Shaping attitudes and the behaviors they inspire is the 'holy grail' of space design." In other words, flexible learning spaces can encourage change, but it isn't the change in and of itself. And regardless of the specifics, all decisions should be made with the best interests of students (not teachers or social media) in mind. Educators shouldn't be designing learning spaces for Pinterest; students should be designing learning spaces for themselves. If we need a structure for students to own this process, we can use some or all of the steps of design thinking to allow students to rethink their entire classroom or certain aspects of it.

David Thornburg's (1999) overarching primordial metaphors for learning spaces can help us to compartmentalize how our classroom could be set up and how different sections can be used. Thornburg believes students should have regularly scheduled time at each of the four spaces. This idea fits perfectly within the context of project based learning. To make this connection, we added an aspect of project based learning in parentheses after each metaphor.

- **Campfire**: Students gather to learn from an expert. The expert does not have to be the teacher (direct instruction).

- **Watering hole**: Students learn from each other, acting as both learner and teacher (peer assessment).

- **Cave**: Students learn by themselves in a quiet and private space (reflection).

- **Life**: Students learn by doing or by applying the knowledge they've acquired (creating a product).

In a PBL environment, there isn't any one perfect way to set up a classroom. Here are five additional considerations.

Desks. In *The Third Teacher* (2010), Dr. Dieter Breithecker, a sports and physical scientist, explains how many schools are failing in this area when he claims, "More than 80 percent of students are not sitting at a workstation that is adjusted to their body size." Countless schools and districts continue to rely on the traditional model of student desks because "that's the way it's always been done" and this idea is rarely framed as a problem that needs fixing. So it stays the same. As an adult, think about how it would feel to spend even one day in a traditional desk. Not comfortable, and not conducive to learning! Alternatives include standing desks, stools, stability balls, beanbags, floor cushions, couches, and ditching desks in favor of tables and chairs.

Student materials. When we start to think about desk alternatives, one of the first questions that always comes up is: What do students do with all their stuff? Rather than problem-solving in isolation or with colleagues, we encourage teachers to collaborate with students on potential solutions. We've never met a class that wasn't capable of housing students' belongings in a central location (e.g., cubbies). Also, most of us work in schools where project based learning is only a part of what we do, so there are times when our materials need to be stored away to make room for other activities. Some of our favorite storage options include laundry baskets (especially stackables), old library shelves, unused lockers, milk crates, and copy paper boxes with lids.

Surfaces. We used to think all student writing had to be done with paper or technology, but this misconception was rectified when we moved to a brand-new school and the back wall of each classroom was lined with a dry-erase board. We regularly took advantage of these walls for student brainstorming, sketching, and posting and rearranging sticky notes. We didn't *look* for excuses to use the walls; the projects and activities came first and we used the boards to enhance this learning. Students also got into the habit of leveraging the boards when needed—no permission required. Alternatives that also work with dry-erase markers include handheld dry-erase boards, dry-erase boards on wheels, dry-erase tables, shower board (a cheap purchase at most hardware stores), and plenty of glass surfaces.

Visual noise. A growing body of research concludes that students are distracted by cluttered and over-decorated classrooms. For example, a Carnegie Mellon University study (Fisher, Godwin, and Seltman, 2014) "found that children in highly decorated classrooms were more distracted, spent more time off-task and demonstrated smaller learning gains than when the decorations were removed." Teachers, especially at the elementary level, should consider this research, but we also shouldn't use it as an excuse to ignore aesthetics altogether. For project based learning, we can have designated wall space (e.g., a bulletin board) for materials related to the current project(s). Working this way helps to establish a routine for everyone involved, and it also gets students into the habit of accessing resources made available to them around the room.

Hallways. More and more, we want to continue to chip away at the "cells and bells" model of students learning in "boxes" and transitioning from one subject to the next at specified times. Taking a look at our hallways can be a way to make this change happen. As Prakash Nair (2014) provocatively announces and then questions, "Hallways remain unused for the majority of the day. ... What if hallways could be turned into a space used for teaching and learning throughout the day?" We have found that ideas flow when we start to view hallways as extensions of our classrooms. This shift can begin by simply putting a couch in a hallway or telling a group of readers they can meet at a table down the hall.

For any school or district tackling flexible learning spaces, if the only change is the furniture, then a whole lot of effort has been spent on nothing more than making students comfortable—which isn't bad—but we can do better. As Rebecca Hare and Bob Dillon (2016) declare, "We are not decorating learning spaces. We are designing them to amplify learning." Our practices and our spaces must go hand in hand.

RELY ON COMMON DENOMINATORS

Think about what you will distribute to students for every project: one-page directions (one-sided), interactive directions, Progress Assessment Tool, folder for all project-related papers, and/or digital hub (website or learning management system) that contains all project-related resources. Working with all of these common denominators creates a routine for teachers, students, and families, and helps to alleviate what could otherwise be a chaotic process.

While some of these materials are discussed throughout the book, for each item, let's take a closer look at frequently asked questions from educators with whom we've interacted. Keep in mind that there's a difference between productive struggle while working toward learning goals and confusion due to poorly planned learning experiences. Attention to detail when we create our materials will help us achieve the former, while also supporting a smoother overall learning experience.

Project directions

When preparing for a PBL unit, we often feel like we have a lot to share with our students about the project before they even get started. For this reason, we must apply a critical eye when we create our directions. Review the components of your project and consider the overall mission, resources students will access, materials students will use, and websites and tools where work will be posted. Decide which information requires directions to keep your students moving forward and self-sufficient, while avoiding step-by-step directions that promote errorless learning. Directions should ultimately address the procedural questions students may have without removing the productive struggle you want them to experience. A project's directions should fit on one side of an 8.5-by-11-inch paper.

Here are eight specific features to always consider when creating project based learning directions.

Umbrella Question. Once you've determined the project's Umbrella Question, make sure it "hits students in the face" wherever they turn for as long as they are engaged in the project. Include it at the top of all project-related materials, such as your directions.

Checkpoints. When students are engaged in project based learning, never wait until the end to see what they've learned. In other words, a final product should never come as a surprise. At certain points, conference with students about their work to approve it before they continue. For example, if you know Step 3 could be a potential sticking point for students, Step 4 in our directions should read: "Teacher conference & approval before moving on." These conferences can be a typical conference, as described in Chapter 3, or a quick check-in to make sure students are on the right track.

Formative assessments. Let students know when formal formative assessments may take place. These assessments are ideal when you place them at hinge points (when there is a clear shift in content).

Summative assessment. Remind students how they will be summatively assessed, if applicable. For example, at the end of your directions, you can include: "At the end of the unit, there will be a culminating test." This reminder is one way to tell students how they will be held accountable for their learning.

Formatting. After typing out your directions, look for opportunities to break down certain portions into numbers (steps) or bullet points (lists). These small tweaks make directions more scannable for students, who will need to follow and use them throughout the project.

Theme-based design. When we first started implementing project based learning, all our directions were quite formal and unimaginative, as they mostly consisted of endless lines of black text on white paper. After considering the ways in which images evoke emotions, we started to make thematic directions, such as a restaurant menu for a restaurant review project, directions in the design of a Lean Cuisine box when learning about plant growth (the Green Cuisine project), and video game graphics when engineering solar-powered cars.

Theme-based fonts. If you create a specific theme for your directions, you will probably want a font that correlates. *Ross:* For example, I used an Angry Birds font to go along with my Angry Animals project. Plenty of websites contain free, instantly recognizable fonts. With a quick Google search, you can find out how to install a font, which you can then use in any application.

Electronically available. If possible, make sure your directions are posted, whether on the classroom website, the project's digital hub (more on digital hubs later in this chapter), in a learning management system, or on Google Drive. This way, students (and possibly families) can access them whenever, wherever. If any of your students lose their directions, rather than having to let you know, they can get their hands on another copy without making a fuss.

Interactive directions

Out of all the materials we consistently use from project to project, this is the most unconventional one, and it is also always met with a huge "aha" whenever we show it during presentations.

ANGRY ANIMALS
HOW CAN THE ANIMALS BE HELPED?

Animal

Animal Background Information

Detailed description of the current problem(s) facing my animal

Teacher Conference & Approval

Detailed description of my plan and how it can help my animal

Action Steps	Timeline: Chronological Order	Who's Responsible?

Teacher Conference & Approval

FIGURE 6.1 - Interactive Directions

Interactive directions are what students fill out as they're working through a project, and Figure 6.1 is an example of what the first page of these directions could look like for the Angry Animals project. As you can see, interactive directions are similar to a project's regular directions, except:

- You create and distribute the document digitally (potentially through Google Docs and Google Classroom). For individual projects, every student receives a copy. For group projects, you can do one copy per group, or have every group member work through their own. Either way, make sure you have editing rights on all documents so you can follow along and insert comments.

- The document mainly consists of helper text (in gray) connected to placeholders (in white) where students can insert text. Create these layouts by inserting and formatting tables and cells in a document. Base the helper text and their placeholders on what every student or group will need to complete, regardless of the process they choose to follow.

Three more points:

- You can insert the checkpoints from the regular directions ("Teacher Conference & Approval").

- Be careful not to over-scaffold. Think of interactive directions as an organization tool with gentle reminders. This keeps students' focus on content and learning goals, while helping you to better keep your finger on the pulse of how students are progressing through their projects.

- If you want to teach students how to organize their work, you can work toward removing this scaffold.

First, create a project's regular directions and Progress Assessment Tool. Then design the interactive directions by looking at the regular directions and asking yourself: "What will all students need to do regardless of the process they choose to follow?" What you don't want is for interactive directions to limit possibilities or stifle student creativity. Also, if done properly, interactive directions should feel like a natural extension of the regular directions; students should be able to easily make connections between the two.

Whenever you roll out a project, make sure your students understand the regular directions and the Progress Assessment Tool, and take time to review the project's digital hub. For interactive directions, because they can be lengthy, you may decide to only go over the steps that students will need during the project's first week or two. Then, as you progress through the project, discuss additional steps, as necessary. This approach helps you avoid the risk of overwhelming students and potentially killing excitement for a project before it truly begins.

Progress Assessment Tool

We've already covered assessment, grading, and the Progress Assessment Tool. However, one question involves the distribution of the tool and students possibly getting confused or overwhelmed by all of its learning targets. This issue can happen if students don't understand the language or fail to grasp the idea that all of the targets need to be hit over time, throughout the project's duration, not immediately.

Let's look at solutions for both of these problems, realizing that for certain students, such as those at the primary level, we may have to tackle both problems at the same time.

The language problem. If language might be an issue, make sure all learning targets are in student-friendly language. If academic language might be an issue, build student background knowledge. You can build this knowledge before you reveal the project, after you reveal the project but before you distribute the Progress

Assessment Tool, or when you give it to students. For additional support, supply students with a glossary of key vocabulary used throughout the project, which encompasses the academic language in the Progress Assessment Tool. Students can use this glossary as a reference to guide their independent work, as opposed to using it as a tool to support the memorization of definitions.

If students struggle with reading, here are four options, some of which you can apply to the creation of a glossary. Choose one or use multiple options in combination with others.

- Minimize text as much as possible.

- Use visuals, such as drawings, photographs, and emojis.

- Link to audio versions of learning targets and success criteria. If you're using a paper version of the Progress Assessment Tool, use QR codes that link to audio files. If you're using a digital version, insert hyperlinks to audio files. Consider making available the audio versions of additional materials, such as project directions.

- For primary grades, combine each learning target with its success criteria to create a target that's a bit more detailed. This allows you to simplify the Progress Assessment Tool by omitting the success criteria column.

The timing problem. This problem can be split into two scenarios. In scenario one, the students are old enough or the content is familiar enough for students to know, either on their own or with a brief explanation by the teacher, that all of the learning targets need to be hit over an extended period. More specifically, they know that even though several learning targets are on their Progress Assessment Tool, not all of them require immediate mastery because they need more instruction from their teacher pertaining to certain targets, they're not currently working on parts of their project that connect to specific targets, or they simply need more time to work. Based on our experiences, students as young as second or third grade can make these connections.

In scenario two, you may worry the students will be overwhelmed when they're not able to mentally sort through the idea that all of the learning targets don't have to be hit immediately. Here are three options for dealing with this.

- Insert a small checkbox next to each learning target, and have students check off each target once they've had the necessary instruction to incorporate it into their projects. (This idea comes from a first grade teacher from Rowayton Elementary School in Norwalk, Connecticut.)

- If the day's work pertains to a specific learning target, have students highlight the target to make connections between what they're doing and what they're supposed to learn. If you're using a paper version of the Progress Assessment Tool, have students place the paper inside a transparent plastic sleeve and then highlight the plastic on top of the target so the highlights can be wiped off. If you're using a digital version, work with students to have them highlight the text electronically.

- Rather than distributing the entire Progress Assessment Tool at once, give students only the learning targets they're incorporating into their projects. For example, students might start with two to three learning targets, with one to two more added at a time until you're done. If you're using a paper version of the Progress Assessment Tool, have students assemble their targets by gluing them to a piece of oak tag or by stapling new targets to the old targets. If you're using a digital version, access students' tools and enter new learning targets when appropriate.

Project folder

Although many schools have recently made a giant leap to paperless classrooms, we still find value in students having certain materials in paper format, especially if they refer to these materials often throughout a project. Toward the beginning of every project, give students a paper copy of the directions and possibly a paper copy of the Progress Assessment Tool. Even if you use a digital version, you can still distribute a paper copy for reference.

In our classrooms, once students received a project's starter materials and we established the Umbrella Question, we gave each student a large piece of oak tag or chart paper that they folded in half and used as a folder for all project-related papers. We then gave them about fifteen minutes to decorate it with the project's title, the Umbrella Question, their name, and project-related designs. Also, for group projects, if students came up with a group name and/or logo, these usually went on the folder as well.

Digital hub

We can also create a one-stop shop for students (and possibly families) to independently access all project-related resources throughout a project's duration. From project to project, we organize each digital hub in a way that feels familiar to students; it helps to divide up the materials into consistent sections.

Here are the sections that are relatively consistent for our projects.

Section 1: Project. We always include one section with materials that encompass the entire project, such as directions, a link to interactive directions, the Progress Assessment Tool, a glossary of terms, and information about a process that will be used during the project (e.g., design thinking or an engineering process).

Section 2: Content. Post materials that are more content-specific, such as handouts from mini-lessons and extended lessons, articles, and videos, in the order in which you teach students the content. If you end up with an overwhelming number of materials, separate them into multiple subsections based on topic. Post all content-specific materials at the start of a project, though you'll probably need to add more materials throughout the project due to students' wants and needs. You might also post all content-specific material when you teach the content.

Section 3: Research. If you will give students links for research, organize the links by topic (and then by medium) in another section.

You can also create additional sections based on your preferences, your students' needs, and the nature of the project. For example, you may want to include a technology section to link to all of the technologies (e.g., websites, apps) students may need to use. For resources that students will need to access across multiple projects (resources on collaboration, public speaking, or slide design), you can post them in a location separate from a specific project, such as on a dedicated website page.

Platforms. Common options include creating a website or blog (Google Sites, Blogger, WordPress.com) with each project having its own dedicated page, or a learning management system (Canvas, Schoology, Google Classroom). The advantage or disadvantage of using a website is that anyone can access the content with the website's link, though certain websites can be password-protected. Meanwhile, learning management systems are closed ecosystems that nobody can accidentally bump into with a Google search, as they can only be accessed with a code or password. Many learning management systems come with options to incorporate interactive content though discussion forums, blogs, and wikis.

A less common option is to upload all materials to Google Drive folders or a similar site, and send students the link. This approach is quick and easy for shorter projects with fewer materials. Finally, in its simplest form, the digital hub can be a cloud-based document with links to materials below each section's heading.

Watch your time

When we roll out a project to students, we're typically not fans of assigning a specific due date, as inflexible scheduling generally prioritizes shallow coverage of content while ignoring the individual needs of students—much like teachers being forced to follow a strict pacing guide. Instead, we would rather give an approximate project duration (e.g., four to six weeks), constantly gauge student learning, and ultimately assign due dates based on student progress. Interim due dates may be for certain steps in the project ("Step 3 should be done by this Friday"), while other deadlines may be set for the entire project ("Everything should be handed in by Monday"). Of course, individuals and groups will learn and complete their projects at different paces, and they may start to hold themselves to their own self-imposed interim due dates. As much as possible, be respectful of these differences when supporting students, assigning due dates, and accepting work.

Problems arise when a project starts to drag on past its intended number of weeks. As a result, it takes much longer than it should for students to demonstrate a deeper understanding of content, and other learning doesn't get the attention it deserves, or it is forgotten completely. These dilemmas are exactly what give project based learning a bad rap, as teachers cry, "There's no time!"

The PBL Paralysis graphic contains four time management tips.

OVERCOMING PBL PARALYSIS

4 TIME MANAGEMENT TIPS

For project based learning newbies, start small, such as by having students all create a similar product (e.g., a podcast), but give them some flexibility in defining the process and what the final product looks like. This approach follows a Product Track.

When planning, less is more. On paper, it always looks exciting when so much is planned: "First students are gonna do *this*, then they're gonna do *this*, then they're gonna do *this*, etc." In reality, projects generally take longer than expected. If we plan too much, we could end up having to choose between pulling the plug on a project in progress or painstakingly limping toward the finish line.

When determining a project's duration, consider these factors: students' strengths and needs, our comfort level, the demands of the content, available resources, the amount of time per day/week dedicated to the project, and the amount of time required for everything else that needs to be taught during the day/year.

Lay out the project, week-by-week, and regularly communicate this schedule with students and possibly post it to the project's digital hub (keeping in mind, things might change).

FINAL THOUGHTS

Erin: Charlie was an eighth grade student during my first year as a middle school assistant principal, and he and I spent a lot of time getting to know each other. Charlie stood out in a traditional classroom because he was the student who couldn't remain in his seat. Often, his interactions with his classmates were awkward. He always forgot to raise his hand before talking, and he never remembered to bring a pencil to class. To some extent, you know students like Charlie.

Something magical happened, however, when Charlie was involved in a design challenge in science class. The mission was to design and construct a flotation device that could hold weight and remain afloat while amassing pennies. Interestingly, all of the behaviors that made Charlie stand out in the standard classroom became assets in this new context. His constant motion made him persistent, and he was dedicated to solving problems that arose. His persistence led to success, which brought his classmates to his side, asking for assistance. This renewed purpose and confidence allowed Charlie to connect with his peers.

The structure and organization of our classrooms matter, as does attention to detail when we roll out project based learning experiences. Every decision we make either fosters or thwarts optimal learning conditions. When we seek to proactively tame the chaos, all individuals achieve more.

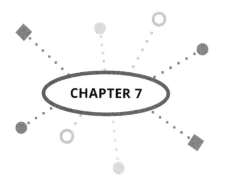

CHAPTER 7

REAL QUESTION:

How Does Inquiry Relate to PBL?

We believe that inquiry—done well—is not the same as turning students loose to discover things to be learned.
— John Larmer, John Mergendoller, and Suzie Boss, authors of *Setting the Standard for Project Based Learning*

Inquiry-based learning can be defined as learning that "starts by posing questions, problems or scenarios—rather than simply presenting established facts or portraying a smooth path to knowledge" (Fang and Logonnathan, 2016). This definition contrasts inquiry with direct instruction; the two are often regarded as the two main methods of teaching. This contrast isn't to say educators must choose between one or the other. As we've discussed, there is certainly room for direct instruction throughout project based learning, and elements of inquiry can be sprinkled throughout direct instruction.

Because inquiry can be applied to everyday teaching and not just entire units by means of project based learning, inquiry serves as an entry point for those who want to eventually implement project based learning. As you read, think about how this chapter applies to project based learning, and also consider how you might bring this same inquiry mindset to the teaching and learning of short-term experiences, such as lessons, activities, and performance tasks.

Many of us made up our minds a long time ago not to dominate class time with direct instruction, the memorization and regurgitation of facts and worksheets. Inquiry is an approach that we can leverage to help form more learner-centered experiences.

However, telling ourselves we need to engage in more inquiry can be comparable to teachers telling students, "Check your work" or "Do a better job collaborating!" The problem is that we want to do better, but we may not necessarily know how, and ambitions in the absence of explicit strategies typically generate anxiety. To avoid these anxieties, and for progress to take place, we need to drill down to the nitty gritty and be as explicit as possible. We need to be explicit about being explicit and use specific strategies to comfortably move forward for the benefit of our students.

REAL ANSWERS:

CONSIDER INQUIRY'S THREE ENTRY POINTS

Educators must approach instructional planning with intentionality. With this in mind, we have found there to be three specific entry points into inquiry. Think of the entry points as ways to frame our thinking as we plan our instruction.

Change the order of instruction

Dan Meyer, a former math teacher and proponent of inquiry-based learning, beautifully gets to the heart of inquiry versus gradual release of responsibility in his one-minute and thirty-seven-second video, "Khan Academy Does Angry Birds" (2012). In the video, his concluding statement is, "When we put the explanation first, we get lousy learning and bored students." The video illustrates how we can move from gradual release to inquiry by simply changing the order of our instruction. Even though gradual release can be appropriate within the context of project based learning, such as during mini-lessons and extended lessons, the issue is when gradual release always replaces project based learning or inquiry as the overall approach.

GRADUAL RELEASE	INQUIRY
1. Get an Explanation	1. Play
2. Play	2. Experiment
3. Experiment	3. Get Feedback
4. Get Feedback	4. Get an Explanation
5. Learn	5. Learn

Meyer, 2012

FIGURE 7.1 - Change the Order of Instruction

Figure 7.1, adapted from the video, contrasts the two approaches. In perhaps more relatable terms, gradual release looks like:

1. **I Do**: Teacher explanation.

2. **We Do**: Explanation continued with student participation.

3. **You Do**: Play and experiment, which more closely resembles students doing the same thing but independently.

In gradual release, feedback generally comes from the teacher, during and/or after play and experiment. In the end, students may gather as a class to discuss what they've learned.

According to the right side of the graphic, inquiry starts with:

1. **You Do**: Play and experiment. During and/or after play and experiment, students can get feedback from the teacher, their peers, and themselves. They may need some background knowledge in advance.

2. **We Do**: Explanation, which occurs when students gather to discuss and clarify what they've uncovered. Explanations come from students with possible teacher facilitation.

3. **I Do**: Learn, which is when the teacher provides direct instruction that hammers home what students should have learned while also potentially rectifying student misconceptions.

As you employ this overall entry point with students, ask yourself: How can I take direct instruction (I do) and move it as far back as possible in the learning process?

Thinking about how this mentality applies to entire units through project based learning, we go back to our question from Chapter 4 regarding whether to teach content proactively: "Will the majority of my students be better off if I simply 'feed them' this information ahead of time, or should I make them work for it?" With gradual release, our default is to use direct instruction proactively in hopes of errorless learning. With inquiry, our default is delaying direct instruction as much as possible to allow for students to learn through productive struggle.

One potential problem with the misuse of gradual release involves students creating the illusion of understanding when they're really just mimicking the teacher. For example, for adding fractions with common denominators, the teacher can force-feed his students the formula: add numerators; denominators stay the same. Then, students can complete numerous problems that are identical to what the teacher showed them (with just the digits changed, of course). In what has been called parrot math, "This approach suggests that children mimic mindlessly what teachers model with the hope that somehow the mimicry will lead to learning. Do parrots understand?" (Van de Walle, 1999). Yes, we may end up with correct answers, but these answers don't necessarily indicate that students understand why they're doing what they're doing, other than to get a good grade.

Finally, we can recall classes during which our teacher announced something like, "As a result of this activity or experiment, you will find out [insert concept]." This model requires students to jump through hoops to arrive at a predetermined outcome. The alternative is an inquiry process that places the teacher explanation after student exploration. Even if students already have an inkling as to what the outcome may be, at least we're not entirely ruining the surprise by giving away the results ahead of time.

Bump into the required learning

This entry point also asks us to reconsider the order of instruction, but from a different angle. Consider these two parallel scenarios.

Scenario 1. Across all subject areas, a sixth grader has learned about fractions, measurement, area, perimeter, and painting. Now that he's comfortable with all of this knowledge, his teacher surprises him by letting him contribute to the construction of a fence for the school's outdoor classroom. (Learn something, now do something with it.)

Scenario 2. A sixth grader would like to contribute to the construction of a fence for the school's outdoor classroom. So, across all subject areas, he works hard to learn about fractions, measurement, area, perimeter, and painting. As a result, he's able to contribute to the fence. (Here's a challenge, now learn what you need to know.)

The second scenario is preferred; the student has incentive to learn because the learning is taking place within an authentic context. Also, for Scenario 2, the student doesn't need to have all prerequisite knowledge before he begins to tackle his challenge; he knows what he has to do, and as a result, he gains the necessary expertise, much like we do in the real world. However, think about how often we've heard, "Students can't learn [insert chapter or topic] until they've learned [insert chapter or topic]." This mentality of students having to learn information in an errorless, linear fashion is entirely inauthentic.

In *Solving 25 Problems in Unit Design* (2015), Wiggins and McTighe echo this sentiment:

> In sports, you don't merely learn rules and basic skills out of context for the first few years before you are allowed on the field to play the game. In art, you don't have to memorize the color wheel and learn about brushes until you are somehow ready to paint or draw.

The alternative is to design learning experiences that will force students to bump into what we want them to learn, and what we want them to learn can easily span across multiple chapters, topics, and even subject areas. Scenario 2 exemplifies how this approach applies to project based learning. If we need our students to learn fractions, measurement, area, perimeter, and painting, we give them a project that will require them to learn this content. To further ensure this "bumping into" happens, we can point students in the direction of the content by including it in the project's directions and assessments.

For individual lessons, the same approach applies. But instead, the "bumping into" takes place across one or two sessions as opposed to the duration of a project. Here are two specific examples.

Example 1. I want my students to learn the parts of a plant cell and to think critically about them. So, after giving students background information on plants and cells, their assignment is to form an argument as to which part of their cells a plant could most likely do without. Each argument must take into consideration all parts of the cell.

Example 2. I want my students to learn the order of operations (PEMDAS) and to be able to apply it to math problems. So, after I briefly tell them about the order of operations, their assignment is to create three problems that would be wrong if solved left to right, as opposed to being solved correctly via the order of operations. Each of the six operations must be used at least once.

We can add direct instruction to the end of each of these examples to help connect student exploration with what we want students to learn.

Uncover understanding

About ten years ago, many of us started to incorporate the Common Core State Standards for Mathematics into our work. As part of this process, we worked with teachers in our district to create Common Core math problems. Generally, we took problems we already had, added the word "Explain" at the end, and then declared them to be Common Core. Of course, looking back, this procedure was entirely ironic. We wanted students to explain their work to demonstrate understanding, yet we as teachers did not understand why we were adding "Explain" to the end of problems.

When we understand, we can think about facts and concepts in a flexible way. We can demonstrate this understanding as we explain, justify, show, apply, and argue. Think of all these verbs as options for students when we ask them to show their work. Meanwhile, rote memorization is characterized by regurgitation—students mimicking the teacher without understanding why they're doing what they're doing (and yes, parrot math is one such example).

Let's apply this contrast to two different scenarios. For each, we'll first look at what it means to teach for rote memorization, then we'll look at what it means to teach for understanding.

Scenario 1

Rote memorization. After Groundhog Day, a bunch of kindergartners are left wondering why some groundhogs saw their shadow and others did not. The teacher explains to them that the results depend on where the groundhog is in relation to the sun.

Understanding. After Groundhog Day, a bunch of kindergartners are left wondering why some groundhogs saw their shadow and others did not. The teacher takes her students on a twenty-minute tour of the outside of the school. During this time, students record when they did and did not see their shadow. Afterward, they head inside for a class discussion, during which they uncover that their shadow (or lack thereof) depends on where they are in relation to the sun. (This activity was facilitated by kindergarten teacher Karen Sterinsky.)

Scenario 2

Rote memorization. It's time to learn about the Bill of Rights. The teacher tells students, "Today we're going to learn about the Bill of Rights." Then she reads one amendment at a time and shares the history behind each one. As she lectures, students take notes.

Later in the week, students take a quiz, matching each amendment number with its description. For each amendment, students are also asked to write a few sentences that explain its history.

Understanding. It's time to learn about the Bill of Rights. The teacher distributes several different scenarios regarding civil rights and actions (e.g., stage a protest in a local park). Students, in small groups, are asked to determine whether or not citizens are allowed to engage in the activity described in the scenario. Once students have sorted through the scenarios, the teacher gives them a copy of the Bill of Rights. She asks students to check their work, using the amendments as evidence to support their decisions. Afterward, everyone comes together as a class to discuss and potentially debate one scenario at a time.

In both scenarios (and countless others, including gradual release), rote memorization can be deceiving as students are able to first appear as if they know what they're doing, but upon being further pressed, reveal their lack of understanding. Meanwhile, while working to build understanding could mean spending more time on the introduction of concepts, we get this time back later on when we don't have to spend as much time reteaching or doing repeated practice.

While the difference between this entry point and the previous is subtle, "bump into" has students thinking, "In order to be successful, I first need to learn ..." Meanwhile, "uncover understanding" has us designing a scenario in which students learn at least one concept through a sort of aha moment.

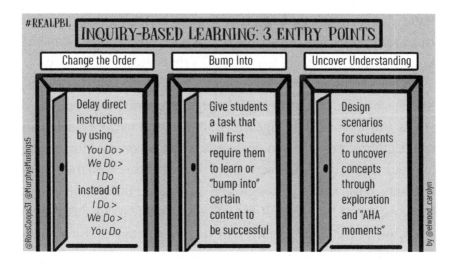

CONSIDER THE DRIVERS OF INQUIRY-BASED LEARNING

In the next four sections, we'll take a look at four considerations when promoting inquiry: the end in mind, questioning, constraints, and productive struggle. These four, along with collaboration (Chapter 5) and feedback (Chapter 2), are, we believe, the six drivers of inquiry-based learning, and the strategies we should always consider when implementing inquiry-based learning. While we don't think every lesson or activity must have all six, we do believe once we (and our students) become comfortable with an inquiry approach, all drivers will naturally find a way into learning experiences on a regular, if not daily, basis.

Begin with the end in mind

During the learning process, students should be aware of their learning targets—one to two for a lesson and eight to ten plus a few High Impact Takeaways for a project based learning experience.

To promote inquiry when working with learning targets, think critically about when they're introduced to students. Revealing the target too early can be comparable to a comedian supplying the punchline to a joke before starting the joke itself; it ruins the suspense. For example, if we're going to teach kindergartners how to add, we wouldn't start by saying, "Today, we're going to learn how to add!" Instead, without even using the term "addition," we'd have students group together manipulatives, then drawings, and finally, numbers. At this point we'd attach the term "addition" to what students are doing, and let them know what they have to do to be successful with it.

Think about letting students dictate how they arrive at the target. We've heard a lot of education talk that declares, "The process is more important than the product" and, "Students should define the process." At times, we think these words are said but not necessarily heard or understood. To clarify such quotes, think of learning as a GPS. In the end, we want all students to arrive at the same destination (learning target), but each student's route (process) will be distinct based on different starting points, wants, and needs. In short, there may be more than one right way for students to arrive at and demonstrate their learning.

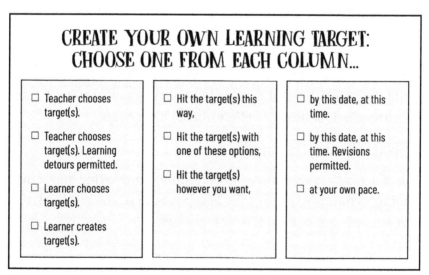

CREATE YOUR OWN LEARNING TARGET: CHOOSE ONE FROM EACH COLUMN...

☐ Teacher chooses target(s).	☐ Hit the target(s) this way,	☐ by this date, at this time.
☐ Teacher chooses target(s). Learning detours permitted.	☐ Hit the target(s) with one of these options,	☐ by this date, at this time. Revisions permitted.
☐ Learner chooses target(s).	☐ Hit the target(s) however you want,	☐ at your own pace.
☐ Learner creates target(s).		

FIGURE 7.2 - Create Your Own Learning Target

This GPS analogy is made more concrete by Figure 7.2, which illustrates the various degrees to which learning targets can impact learning. From top to bottom, choices range from most restrictive to least restrictive. For example, after choosing one from each column, we can end up with, "Teacher chooses target(s). Hit the target(s) this way, by this date, at this time." Here, we're one-size-fits-all without student choice. The other extreme is, "Learner creates target(s). Hit the target(s) however you want, at your own pace." This path resembles personalized learning.

While the graphic illustrates the flexibility of learning targets through various combinations, not all possibilities are covered because we can blur the lines between what's listed. For example, for the second column, the teacher could say, "Hit the target(s) with one of these options, but you can also come up with something on your own, pending teacher approval." Our intention wasn't to generate a graphic that fills every nook and cranny, but rather to provide key options that hammer home the ideas that learning targets can be leveraged to support anything from direct instruction to personalized learning, and oftentimes, examining progressive practices through the lens of learning targets can make our lives easier.

Finally, the graphic lends itself to short-term learning through lessons, activities, or performance tasks, but for entire units, we could create an identical graphic by swapping out learning targets for Umbrella Questions or High Impact Takeaways.

Prioritize questioning

When looking to promote more inquiry, improving our questioning techniques is one of the first places to start. Two quick tips that have guided our work in this area are:

- We formulate questions based on how we think students will respond to them. A question is only as good as the reactions it elicits.

- The endgame is students asking and exploring their own questions. But this doesn't happen by accident.

Here are three ways to support questioning and inquiry.

Bloom's Taxonomy and Webb's Depth of Knowledge. Bloom's Taxonomy, originally created by Benjamin Bloom in 1956, includes six levels: knowledge, comprehension, application, analysis, synthesis, and evaluation. In 2001, the taxonomy was revised by two of his former students, Anderson and Krathwohl, to instead include six verbs in order of increasing complexity: remember, understand, apply, analyze, evaluate, and create. Another option, Webb's Depth of Knowledge (DOK), was created by Norman Webb in 1997. The DOK contains four levels of increasing complexity: recall, basic application of skill or concept, strategic thinking, and extended thinking.

These tools can help us intentionally craft questions, activities, tasks, and even entire projects based on how complex we want them to be. However, we must also consider our students' prior knowledge; how students will respond to our questions, activities, tasks, and projects; and the context in which we're presenting what we have planned. All of these factors will influence the learning that takes place. Also, we need to stop entertaining the idea that students should be learning at the highest level, all the time. As Karin Hess (2018) explains, "This devalues the role of foundational and conceptual understanding in laying the groundwork for deeper thinking."

Finally, we can also consider having our students use these tools to assist them in asking (and then exploring) their own questions.

Less is more. *Ross:* I can still vividly recall a professional learning session I helped facilitate when I was a fourth grade teacher. The session was driven by the Umbrella Question: "How can fewer questions lead to a deeper understanding?" From the district reading program, teachers analyzed half of a story along with the ten publisher-created questions that came with it. In diving into these questions, teachers were led to uncover that no higher-order thinking had to take place for them to be answered. So, to replace the ten questions, teachers came up with two to three questions that prompted higher-order thinking and encompassed the majority of the content from the ten questions, and a thinking routine that would allow for students to explore these new questions. A routine was necessary because if we asked "thick" questions the same way we asked "thin" questions, we would most likely continue to get shallow answers. We were creating the conditions for higher-order thinking to occur.

Students, not teachers, should be asking the majority of questions. But this is easier said than done. We want students asking thick questions that can lead to meaningful learning. Rather than telling students what these thick questions involve, we can have them uncover these features. Here's one activity we have done with our students:

1. The teacher informs students that the difference between thick questions and thin questions is that thick questions require more thinking.

2. Individually, students read a text. Whenever they have an interesting question, they write it on a sticky note and stick it in the margin, next to the part of the story to which it applies.

3. In groups, after reading the story, students read each other's notes and then work together to line them up from thickest to thinnest (on a wall or across desks).

4. Everyone comes together as a class to share their questions/notes and decisions. Through discussion, they create a list of thick question features.

Thick question features may include: They lead to interesting conversations or arguments, they make us think about a whole lot of information, and they can never truly be solved (much like Umbrella Questions). If we want to do a similar activity but give students more scaffolding, we can first tell them these features, or something similar, and then have them find and discuss questions that fit these descriptions. We can also modify this activity to make it work with other mediums, such as video and audio.

The PBL Paralysis graphic explains three more ways we can get students to ask their own questions.

We also recommend looking into the Question Formulation Technique. In their book, *Make Just One Change*, Dan Rothstein and Luz Santana establish this protocol. Using this technique, students are presented with a prompt, which they respond to with their own questions. Students then refine their questions, prioritize those that are most pertinent, and evaluate their work. Their final questions serve as a springboard into course content.

Student questioning is a non-negotiable of inquiry. Students should not only be asking their own questions, but also get the opportunity to explore and act upon their curiosities. For an in-depth guide to questioning in the classroom, see *Hacking Questions: 11 Answers that Create a Culture of Inquiry in Your Classroom* (2019) by Connie Hamilton (published by Times 10 Publications).

OVERCOMING PBL PARALYSIS

3 WAYS TO GET STUDENTS TO ASK QUESTIONS

ONE

We react appropriately to students' questions.

Students may be conditioned to believe their questions won't matter if they don't align with what they're learning (or anything else in our curriculum). When we react in a genuine way to our students' questions, regardless of what they may be, we send the message we value their unique curiosities and interests. As a result, even more questions are likely to emerge.

TWO

We let students use their questions.

Of course, these questions won't mean much if we don't let students act upon them. In some instances, if we're not taking too much of a learning detour, we can immediately tackle certain questions. In other instances, students can document their questions (in a journal, on a classroom parking lot, etc.), and then look into them during time set aside for such inquiries, such as Genius Hour.

THREE

We ask our own questions.

But, if students are the only ones asking and exploring questions, they may be led to believe they're playing the game of school. Instead, as students ask questions, we can ask questions of our own. As students dive into their questions, we can do the same, while also facilitating student learning. When we share our questions with our students, we're modeling the types of questions we want them to be asking.

#REALPBL

Leverage constraints

In *LAUNCH* (2016), John Spencer and A.J. Juliani proclaim, "The myth is that creativity is the outcome of complete freedom. The reality is quite the opposite. Creativity often stems from pain and conflict. It starts with problems we encounter and situations where time, resources, and information are limited." In other words, we're thinking inside the box. For any given situation, the box's characteristics are determined by the constraints—limitations or restrictions—with which we must deal. To illustrate this point, Spencer and Juliani rehash the Apollo 13 story of NASA engineers literally fitting a square peg into a round hole in order to save astronauts' lives. Of course, there were other constraints, such as a time limit (before long, the astronauts would run out of oxygen), only having certain supplies on hand, and having to transmit the final plans to the space shuttle.

JUST BECAUSE YOU'RE TEACHING THE SAME PROJECT AS THE TEACHER NEXT DOOR DOESN'T MEAN STUDENTS FROM BOTH CLASSES ARE GETTING THE SAME EXPERIENCE.

Let's take a look at how constraints can be leveraged to promote inquiry. We'll do this by examining two different ways to facilitate an egg drop project. Yes, *that* egg drop project, in which students are charged with designing a protective packaging for an egg in hopes of it surviving a drop from up high.

Experience 1: Space camp egg drop. *Ross:* As an eight-year-old at space camp, I absolutely loved partaking in the egg drop, which is one reason I still remember it. More or less, the process looked like this: Campers were given a whole bunch of materials to use to build protective egg packaging however they wanted. My product ended up including an empty Triscuit box, loads of packing peanuts, packaging tape, and a bit more. And my egg survived the drop from the top of the camp's building!

Experience 2: Fourth grade egg drop. I facilitated this experience as a fourth grade teacher. My students took an approach that blended design thinking with the scientific method. Here are the approximate steps that we followed:

1. The entire class worked together to uncover the attributes of ideal egg packaging from the consumer's point of view: protective, small size, insulated, and attractive.

2. In groups, students researched, planned, and recorded how their packaging would satisfy each attribute. Then they sketched their packaging, conferred with the teacher, and got approval before moving on.

3. Groups engineered their packaging using materials from the classroom and/or their homes, iterating as necessary as they went along.

4. Products were dropped from the school's roof, and then students reflected upon the entire process.

While there's nothing technically wrong with a fun activity like the space camp egg drop, slightly tweaking the project's directions could get campers (and students) thinking on a much more critical level. As an eight-year-old, I had the simple task of building packaging to protect an egg, and really not much thought and effort had to go into it other than piecing together materials and inserting an egg into the middle of it all. But if we add a constraint or two, like we did in Experience 2 with the attributes of ideal packaging, we are now engineering. We want these constraints to promote inquiry, but we also want them to represent what an authentic product includes.

The differences between the two activities are worth noting, as they demonstrate how the same project or activity can look entirely different based on the teacher's decisions (some subtle, some not so much) during the project planning process. In fact, on several occasions, we have seen an entire grade level of teachers agree to roll out the same project, but unbeknownst to them, the learning that transpired from classroom to classroom was almost entirely different. Most of the time, these differences were due to the different comfort levels of teachers when designing inquiry-based experiences and the willingness of these teachers to let go and allow students to be at the center of the learning. Either way, just because you're teaching the same project as the teacher next door doesn't mean students from both classes are getting the same experience.

At a more basic level, here's how we can use constraints to push student thinking during everyday lessons:

- How could you calculate 34 x 3 if the 3 button on your calculator was broken?

- Without using technology, how could you best predict tomorrow's weather?

- The art room is out of blue paint, and you need to paint a sky. What do you do?

- Do a research project. Don't use websites.

Embrace productive struggle

As students work toward learning goals, productive struggle is the main difference between hands-on learning and minds-on learning. For the most part, our goal is the latter.

In *Hacking Project Based Learning*, we assert, "Through this productive struggle, students work to *uncover* understandings of content as opposed to serving as bystanders while the teacher *covers* curriculum through lectures, worksheets, and disconnected tasks."

However, telling students they shouldn't take the shortest and easiest path from point A to point B is baffling for many educators. According to Dr. John Van de Walle (2018):

> It is hard to think of allowing—much less planning for—the children in your classroom to struggle. Not showing them a solution when they are experiencing difficulty seems almost counterintuitive. If our goal is relational understanding, however, the struggle is part of the learning, and teaching becomes less about the teacher and more about what the children are doing and thinking.

To help create a culture of productive struggle and to emphasize the fact that iteration is all around us, we told students the story of the original iPhone prior to it being released. In this instance, an angry Steve Jobs noticed that the plastic screen of a "ready to ship" iPhone became noticeably scratched when placed in his pocket along with other items, such as keys. As a result, with six weeks to go until the product was announced, the screens had to change from plastic to glass. In the end, the phone underwent countless trials and errors before it reached its present state (Blodget, 2012). When working with younger students, especially, we need to bring these processes to light to remind them that productive struggle isn't just the norm; it's necessary.

Here are two practical tips to keep in mind when allowing for productive struggle.

Let students (and maybe families) know it's supposed to happen. Unless we're teaching in a school with an explicit focus on inquiry and project based learning, there's a strong chance our students will interpret productive struggle as just struggle. In other words, they'll think there's something wrong because they're not getting it. So, beforehand, let them know that struggle and iteration are a part of the learning process. (The Steve Jobs story helps to communicate this message.) Then, support students along the way by reacting accordingly to their mistakes and regularly offering prompts and feedback, not answers. In *Creativity, Inc.* (2014), Ed Catmull tells us, "When experimentation is seen as necessary and productive, not as a frustrating waste of time, people will enjoy their work—even when it is confounding them."

We can always give, but we can't take away. Once we give our students overly detailed (possibly step-by-step) directions, we've let the cat out of the bag. Our students will probably know exactly what to do and inquiry will be nonexistent. Instead, we can err on the side of caution by asking ourselves: "What do I need to give my students to maximize inquiry and creativity while ensuring an unreasonable level of frustration will not be reached?" Here, the goal is to give students "Goldilocks Directions," or directions that aren't too easy, aren't too hard, but are just right. We want the majority of students to experience productive struggle. For those who are struggling unproductively, filter in additional directions, varying from student to student or group to group as needed.

FINAL THOUGHTS

When considering direct instruction and inquiry, we have found that the majority of teachers generally favor one approach and stick with it for most of their teaching, and if/when teachers make the shift to inquiry, they never go back. This was certainly true for us. Since we made this transition, whenever we plan our lessons and units, we ask ourselves, almost subconsciously, how we can infuse inquiry into the teaching and learning.

Nevertheless, we don't have to choose between direct instruction and inquiry, as both can coexist for the benefit of our students. But we do believe inquiry should be more pervasive. Grant Wiggins (2014) extends this sense of urgency by claiming, "If the aim of education is to produce autonomous and inquisitive students, then it seems plausible to argue that student inquiry (and thus, student questions) should drive curriculum."

Inquiry serves as a project based learning entry point because it can be integrated into lessons, activities, and performance tasks, and not just entire units. Once we become comfortable with applying inquiry on a smaller scale, we can transition to leveraging it across entire units through project based learning. Others may refer to these units as inquiry-based units, curricular inquiries, or something else. But, no matter what we call it, common language is important as it helps us avoid confusion while promoting collaboration and a clear vision.

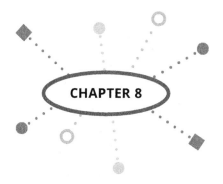

CHAPTER 8

REAL QUESTION:

How Do I Get Started with PBL?

You can't be that kid standing at the top of the waterslide, overthinking it. You have to go down the chute.
— TINA FEY, ACTRESS

E RIN: ONE YEAR, while working with a student teacher in my fifth grade classroom, I came upon an interesting realization. As the student teacher began to take over more of the instructional load, he integrated some of my classroom management techniques, including my routine for gaining student attention before giving a direction. This routine, which felt natural for me and my students, always seemed to fall short for the student teacher. He struggled to gain student attention, and eventually, he ended up raising his voice. During one of our weekly reflection sessions, I asked, "How does it feel when you implement that routine?" His honest response: "It works for you, so it should work for me, right?"

At the time, I didn't fully appreciate the magnitude of the mentality "it works for others, so it should work for me." To this day, we are continually surprised by the persistent assumption that copy and paste is the way to go. One-size-fits-all doesn't work for students, and it doesn't work for educators. Such is the case for those of us looking to get started with project based learning. There is no single entry point; we must find our own. The integration of project based learning emerges on a continuum, and our location on this continuum is not fixed. We can slide back and forth based on students' strengths and needs, our comfort level, the demands of the content, and available resources.

Educators are usually surprised when they realize there are multiple ways to get started with project based learning, that they've already gotten started and just don't know it, or that project based learning isn't all or nothing (you're either doing it or you're not).

Let's take a look at some of the ways you can get started.

REAL ANSWERS:

START WITH ONE OF THE THREE TRACKS

In *Hacking Project Based Learning*, we introduced three tracks that serve as markers on the PBL continuum. When we share these options with teachers, they often ask us which track they should use. No one likes the answer, "It depends!" However, making this choice depends on multiple factors. We don't believe a prescriptive approach to project based learning exists. Instead, we offer additional considerations to be used in decision-making.

Product Track

The Product Track is a potential starting point if you or your students have limited experience with project based learning, or if this is the first time you and your students are engaging in project based learning together. In the Product Track, students create a product(s) or contribute to an event. For clarity, this is different from a traditional project because even though all students may create or contribute to something similar, they can exercise their creativity to own the process, and all learning is done with the product or event in mind, as opposed to it being tacked on after the learning as an extra.

The Product Track can be differentiated based on how the product or event is determined. Sometimes, the teacher chooses the final outcome. In other circumstances, the teacher may frame the unit, offer options, and allow students to select their product or event. As another possibility, the teacher may frame the unit and allow students to come up with products or events of their own.

Some examples from the Product Track include:

- Movie trailer predicting a book's sequel
- Monument illustrating a historic person or time period
- Healthy smoothie to enhance quality of life
- Debate on the effectiveness of homework
- Performance of skits for students in other classes

Problem Track

The Problem Track frames the learning experience around addressing a shared concern. This track is ideal if you or your students have identified an authentic issue that your class can address. Solving a problem offers an additional layer of motivation. Getting involved in fixing a real issue is often the extra inspiration a group of students needs to engage in courageous work.

The Problem Track also allows for differentiation in approach. The problem can be identified by the teacher, or the teacher can introduce a topic and ask students to identify an associated problem. If multiple problems arise, the class may decide to tackle one problem together, or the teacher may allow for each student or group to address their own problem.

Some examples from the Problem Track include:

- Student desks are uncomfortable
- It takes too long to get through the lunch line
- Low circulation rates at a local library need to be addressed
- A local diner (a neighborhood favorite) needs remodeling
- Endangered animals need help to survive

Open-Ended Track

Typically considered the least restrictive option, open-ended project based learning invites students to demonstrate their learning in any way that works for them, as long as they're working toward the designated High Impact Takeaways and learning targets. This approach to a unit is usually best suited for teachers and students who have experience with project based learning. In a class of thirty students, with everyone involved in their own project, the teacher will need to feel comfortable having students take multiple paths to reach a similar destination. Students will also need to feel comfortable with the available options and resources so they can explore with minimal direction.

Optionally, for additional support, the teacher may consider providing students with an Umbrella Question that's either given to them or that they create together, or some written direction. If the teacher gives a form of guidance, they may want to guide students to explore an abstract question, conduct an investigation, or take a position on an issue (Larmer, Mergendoller, and Boss, 2015).

START WITH HANDS-ON, TRANSITION TO MINDS-ON

When students work toward learning goals, productive struggle is the main difference between hands-on learning and minds-on learning. While our goal is frequently the latter, this transition can be easier said than done. Just as old-school projects can be a starting point for project based learning, there's also nothing wrong with some hands-on learning, as long as we're looking to move toward minds-on.

Ross: Let's take a look at how I transitioned from hands-on to minds-on with solar-powered cars, while keeping in mind that these same ideas and steps could be applied across countless products and contexts.

The starting point

I originally purchased a classroom ten-pack of solar-powered car kits. According to the parts list, each kit included the following: coroplast frame, push pin, screw eyes (5), wood block (2), shorter axle shaft, longer axle shaft, tweazle stick, wooden wheels (5), sandpaper, tubing, pulley, motor, motor mounting clip, elastic bands (2), and solar panel with alligator clip test leads.

Each of the ten kits also included explicit step-by step directions—nineteen steps in all for users to piece together their cars in an errorless fashion. These directions also had photographs. And, just in case, they also included a link to a video that demonstrated exactly how the directions should be followed.

The transition

To encourage inquiry-based learning and to place the engineering process in the hands of students as much as possible, I decided they would not be receiving all of the supplies I had purchased. So, I asked myself: "What do I need to give my students to maximize inquiry and creativity while ensuring an unreasonable level of frustration will not be reached?"

After working through this question for quite some time with Matt Snyder, the school's custodian, I decided that the students would be provided with the following:

- One solar panel with alligator clip test leads
- One motor
- Four wooden wheels
- One shorter axle shaft
- One longer axle shaft
- Four screw eyes
- Also, students were permitted to incorporate their own supplies

Take a moment to contrast this list with what was included in the original directions.

To further the engineering process, as opposed to open-ended building with no constraints or goals, the students were made aware of five potential class awards they could receive for their final car or product: most creative, best designed, most eco-friendly, fastest, and highest speed per dollar. Each group was asked to select two, explain their strategy for winning each one, and then blueprint and design their cars with their chosen awards in mind.

The new directions included the following components:

- A blueprint, drawn in detail with all parts labeled
- Explanations and mini-blueprints for individual systems within the car (e.g., making sure the wheels turn once the motor is powered)
- Documentation of the main problems and solutions that arise during engineering
- Budget documentation
- Reflection, with an emphasis on how successful or unsuccessful each group was in winning their targeted awards

In the end

To preview the productive struggle that would take place, I shared my planning process and intentions with the students when I handed over the challenge. This transparency helped students understand that productive struggle and iteration were a designed part of the learning.

Finally, if we want to add to this activity until we have a project based learning experience, we can integrate our elements of project based learning from Chapter 1: High Impact Content and Supporting Content, High Impact Takeaways, Umbrella Question, learning targets, Progress Assessment Tool, and more.

START WITH STUDENT PUBLISHING

Once again, in *Hacking Project Based Learning*, we originally revealed how project based learning is a series of best practices joined together. These practices, many of which can be used with or without project based learning, include, but are not limited to: establishing a culture of inquiry and creativity, designing flexible learning spaces, teaching collaboration skills, facilitating student self-assessment, elevating student learning with conferencing and feedback, integrating direct instruction, using formative assessments to drive instruction, student publishing, and student reflection. Any one of these practices can serve as an entry point into project based learning. One of these practices that we believe deserves more attention (in this book and in education) is student publishing, which, with internet access, represents an easy way to start breaking down the walls of our classrooms.

> **WITHHOLDING PUBLISHING FROM STUDENTS WHO ARE STRUGGLING IS THE EQUIVALENT OF SAYING, "IT IS A PRIVILEGE TO BE TAUGHT IN AN EXCITING, AUTHENTIC WAY."**

In November 2011, Alan November, an education technology leader, gave a TEDx Talk at a New York event. During his talk, he tells a story (which begins at the seven-minute, thirty-second mark) about how his daughter discovered a young writer who had a significant following because of her work on fanfiction.net—writings in which she expanded upon the work of J.K. Rowling by writing her own original Harry Potter stories. November met the young author and learned that she was struggling in school. He asked her why she struggled in school when she was experiencing such great success with the online writing platform. She told him:

> I've decided that when I wake up, I have to make a decision now. Do I write for my teachers or do I publish for the world? That's a really important decision. And more and more the answer is, publish for the world.

The catch is that this story took place in 2003 before many kids had discovered the global capacity for publishing their writing. Now students have discovered that they can have a global voice, and we need to let them publish—if not for the world, then at least for their peers.

So, what comes first, the basics or the publishing? In other words, should students have to master the basics before they are allowed to publish? Or, can they learn *while* publishing? In our minds, without hesitation, the answer is the latter. As, ultimately, withholding publishing from students who are struggling is the equivalent of saying, "It is a privilege to be taught in an exciting, authentic way."

Publishing platforms

Choose publishing platforms with intentionality. We believe in using authentic tools that are commonly used outside of school, as opposed to tools that have been made for school. The PBL Paralysis graphic explains three reasons why.

OVERCOMING PBL PARALYSIS
3 REASONS TO USE REAL WORLD TECHNOLOGY TOOLS

Teaching digital citizenship is a non-negotiable.

If we're having students leverage "safe" made for school technology because we're afraid of what might happen, they're missing out on valuable learning opportunities. Experiences with authentic tools allow for students to apply what they've learned in settings that very much mimic the real world, and at the same time we're present to turn mistakes into beneficial lessons.

Teaching entrepreneurialism or the entrepreneurial spirit is quickly becoming a non-negotiable.

Not only should students be learning how to do their work, they should be learning and experiencing how to share and market their creations. In time, students can be creating and promoting their own businesses, gaining loyal audiences with podcasts, publishing and marketing eBooks, etc. All of this is made possible with an authentic platform.

Your digital footprint is your new résumé.

If our students are applying for colleges without digital footprints, we're doing them a disservice. We need to make sure our students are *searchable* - giving them a leg up on the competition due to their digital footprints. Most made for school technologies don't show up in search engines. And, we want students to get acquainted with the tools they'll most likely employ once they leave school.

We'll refrain from mentioning specific technologies.
The tools will change; our philosophy will not.

#REALPBL

We do believe the conversation should at least start with authentic technologies. There may be limiting factors, such as high costs, a tool's complexity, and age restrictions, but we are limiting the possibilities if we play it safe and only consider what's made for school.

At the very least, let students publish.

START WITH STUDENT CHOICE

In the Introduction, we discussed engagement versus relevance and the ways in which student choice can help us achieve relevance. Student choice can also serve as an entry point into project based learning, as putting choices in the hands of students is a natural way to transition from old-school projects to PBL. However, it can be challenging to infuse student choice into our lessons and units. Based on our experience, it's easy for teachers to quickly and wrongfully assume that their students' learning is brimming with choice, when in reality, the learning is more about what the teacher wants, not what the students need. (And yes, we have been guilty of these same mistakes.)

On several occasions, we have worked with teachers to incorporate more student choice into their instruction. Here are directions for two activities that you can use to do that, and even if you're not going to facilitate one of these activities, some of the steps (e.g., the T-Chart idea in Step 2) can help you think critically about your own work.

Shorter activity

1. Watch and then discuss the video "10 Ways to Empower Students With Choice" by John Spencer.

2. Choose a project you have already facilitated that you would like to revise. With your project in mind, fill out a T-Chart. The left side, titled "Teacher

Choice," should contain the teacher choices that took place during the project. The right side, titled "Student Choice," should contain the student choices that took place during the project.

3. Analyze and discuss your T-Charts and projects, using the following prompts:

   - Overall, what do you notice? Does anything surprise you?

   - How could you provide more student choice within your project? Think about content (what students learn), process (how students learn), product (evidence of learning), and environment (how the classroom is structured) (Tomlinson, 2017).

   - What are your reservations for providing more student choice?

4. Based on your discussion, what are your next steps?

Longer activity

1. Watch and then discuss the video "10 Ways to Empower Students With Choice" by John Spencer.

2. Choose a project you have already facilitated that you would like to revise. With your project in mind, fill out a T-Chart. The left side, titled "Teacher Choice," should contain the teacher choices that took place during the project. The right side, titled "Student Choice," should contain the student choices that took place during the project.

3. In groups, analyze and discuss each other's T-Charts and projects, using the following prompts:

- Overall, what do you notice? Does anything surprise you?

- Looking at everyone's examples of student choice, are there ways you could group them into categories? What commonalities exist?

- For those in your group, what suggestions do you have for providing more student choice in their projects? Think about content (what students learn), process (how students learn), product (evidence of learning), and environment (how the classroom is structured) (Tomlinson, 2017).

4. Have a whole-group discussion on the previous prompts, which should also lead into a discussion regarding why student choice is important.

5. Revise your project while looking to emphasize student choice more heavily. As you're revising, consider the following questions:

- Will students be designing a product? Solving a problem? Open-ended? Something else?

- As a result of the project, what do you want students to understand?

- How will students be assessed and possibly graded?

- For the lessons that take place within the context of your project, what content will need to be addressed, and how will it be addressed?

6. Afterward, share the following:

- Briefly, what was your "before" project? What is your "after" project? How do they contrast?

- What new opportunities are there for student choice? How do you think these opportunities will benefit your students?

7. Provide peer feedback.

What can make student choice so effective is its simplicity, and the fact that it is a term that doesn't need explaining to educators, students, and families. With so many approaches to teaching and learning, an extra hurdle exists when we need to establish what they truly are in order to get the most out of them. It's an extra hurdle that can easily turn off participants when they have to deal with more unfamiliar jargon. As we saw in Chapter 1 with project based learning, this idea of defining can be hard for individuals, and formulating a common definition can be even more difficult for organizations.

Student choice, however, doesn't present this barrier, as it's self-explanatory; common language already exists. We can skip the *what* and get straight to the *why* and the *how*. And, by starting with student choice, we can then seamlessly transition into project based learning, which is what the longer activity accomplishes.

START WITH AN EXISTING PROJECT

Another entry point worth mentioning is repackaging an old-school project as a project based learning experience, as detailed in Chapter 1. As we work with educators on this transition, a favorite activity is titled "How Might I Redesign a Crappy Project?" *Ross:* During this time, participants are asked to dissect a project I facilitated as a fourth grade teacher, in which all students created a brochure for the East Region of the United States. Of course, at the time, I thought the project was cutting edge, and I can recall bragging about it to everyone who would listen. But, looking at it now, as I designed the project, my thought process very closely mimicked the first narrative from Chapter 1, and the results show in what I now believe to be a crappy project.

As participants dissect the project and its rubric, they do so through the lens of six questions. These questions work with countless projects, including your own, and also work with pre-made projects we find on the internet or from colleagues.

1. **When does the learning occur?** Learning should occur throughout the project, as opposed to the project being added on after the "real learning" has taken place. This contrast is often referred to as the project being the main course instead of the dessert.

2. **What relevance does the project have on students' lives?** Are we settling for engagement when we can do better?

3. **To what extent can the learning be personalized?** If we were to take all of the choices made throughout the project and categorize them as teacher choice or student choice, what would we uncover? How might we then put more choices in the hands of our students?

4. **Who assesses the learning?** Ideally, we want students to be able to self-assess throughout their learning.

5. **Who is the audience?** With certain technologies at our disposal, there's no reason why all work should be created for an audience of one: the teacher. When students work with a certain audience in mind, beyond the teacher, their work is that much more authentic.

6. **Anything else you'd like to add?**

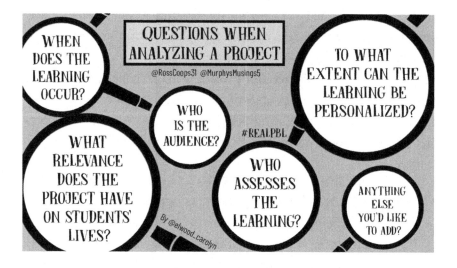

The activity serves two specific purposes other than helping to transition from projects to project based learning. First, being transparent about our journey makes us more relatable, while hopefully encouraging others to be willing to learn with us. As a facilitator of professional learning, it's easy to show up with the attitude, "I've done all of the work and research; *this* is how things should be done." Showing the mistakes we've made along the way groups all of us together as educators who simply want to do better by our students, and everyone is able to see their mistakes as part of a universal process instead of something that's exclusive to them.

Second, we use our own project so others don't have to use theirs. We can't tell you how many times we've done this activity and overheard a participant say something to the effect of, "This looks like one of my projects." By throwing our own work under the bus, we're meeting others where they are and moving them forward without directly criticizing their current practices.

When we spend time in classrooms, working with teachers and students to transition from projects to project based learning, a question we can regularly ask students is: What are you learning and why are you learning it? When answers relate to specific technologies or tools, products, following steps, or doing well on a test, the teaching and learning is perhaps in the wrong place, and we most likely have a project on our hands. In contrast, we would rather have students' answers relate to learning goals and how the learning is relevant to them on a personal level.

START WITH GENIUS HOUR

Also referred to as 20 Percent Time and Passion Projects, Genius Hour is based on the beliefs that 1) students learn best when they have autonomy over their learning, and 2) we need to make time at school for students to explore their passions, as opposed to them playing the game of school while they're with us and then going home to experience their real learning. In the words of Austin Kleon (2012), "School is one thing. Education is another. The two don't always overlap." Our job is to make sure this overlap happens as much as possible.

Genius Hour involves students interacting with topics or exploring questions of their choosing through research, taking action (often beyond classroom walls), and then possibly presenting on their work. As topics are based on student choice, there's no guarantee there will be connections to content standards (e.g., narrative writing, fractions, Civil War), but there can always be connections to process standards (e.g., research, problem solving, collaboration). Sometimes, after students have done much of their work, teachers will collaborate with them to make explicit connections between student accomplishments and content and process standards.

In *Genius Hour* (2017), Andi McNair provides a straightforward six-step process (the 6 Ps) for Genius Hour:

1. **Passion**: What do you want to learn about? What do you think is interesting? What can you get excited about?

2. **Plan**: Who will be your outside expert? What materials will you need to complete the project? What will you need to do each day to reach your goals?

3. **Pitch**: How will you share your idea with the class? How will you get us on board?

4. **Project**: It's time to dive in! What do you need to do today to move forward with your project? What are you creating, making, or designing?

5. **Product**: What did you create? What can you show us to demonstrate your learning?

6. **Presentation**: How do you plan to share your learning? Can you share your idea or project with others? What tools will you use to make your presentation engaging for the audience?

This is a process that the teachers with whom we've worked have found helpful. Of course, there are countless ways to tackle Genius Hour. We recommend having students frame their passion with a question to 1) promote inquiry, and 2) help them make their work actionable. For example, for McNair's first step, instead of choosing to focus on "baking," students can deepen their exploration with a targeted question: "How might I bake with the fewest ingredients possible?"

Project based learning always connects to content standards (and process standards) through teaching, learning, and assessment. For teachers, especially those who have less experience with project based learning, designing these types of experiences can be tricky and possibly intimidating. In addition, teachers may not be comfortable with its learner-centered nature.

Genius Hour can serve as a comfortable entry point into project based learning. Genius Hour is easier to plan for as it doesn't come with the constraint of having to connect to content standards, and because it doesn't require connections to these standards, it's a low-risk, high-reward means of putting students at the center of the learning. Also, because Genius Hour honors students' interests over curriculum, we can leverage this approach to get students excited about owning their learning.

Rather than Genius Hour serving as an entry point, it can run simultaneously with project based learning. *Ross:* In my fourth grade classroom, project based learning took place continuously throughout the year, and Genius Hour happened almost every Thursday for about forty-five minutes. Many teachers facilitate Genius Hour on a regular basis (such as weekly), regardless of what else may be transpiring in their classrooms.

FINAL THOUGHTS

We have worked with many teachers, schools, and districts who begin the PBL journey by taking one to two units and transforming them into project based learning—either as a self-imposed goal or as a school or district goal. In fact, as teachers participating in our district's PBL initiative, we were asked to implement and then share just one PBL unit at some point during the upcoming school year.

While we used to agree with this approach, it can present two problems. First, it establishes the same goal for everyone regardless of their current practices and knowledge. While some may be ready to implement a full project based learning experience, others may feel it's too much too soon. This is when the multiple entry points can help.

Second, we get better by making mistakes, learning from our

mistakes, and then applying what we've learned. But, if we only facilitate one to two projects a year, we're forced to wait until the next year to apply our learning. As a result, our learning curve can be slow and arduous, and we don't develop expertise as quickly as we should.

As an alternative, rather than looking to implement one to two projects, try to implement two to three PBL components, such as flexible learning spaces and student publishing; implement four to five shorter projects; or engage students in at least two months of project based learning. (Numbers and durations will vary based on context.) Either way, you're creating the conditions to not just learn from your mistakes, but also repeatedly apply what you've learned through experiences, and in a timely manner. And for students who aren't used to project based learning, shorter projects can be less overwhelming.

This is the same approach taken by Tom Kelley and David Kelley in their work with design thinking. In *Creative Confidence* (2013), they reveal:

> In our classes and workshops, we first ask people to work through quick design challenges. ... Building confidence through experience encourages more creative action in the future, which further bolsters confidence. For this reason, we frequently ask students and team members to complete multiple quick design projects rather than one big project, to maximize the number of learning cycles.

No matter where we are with project based learning, this maximizing of learning cycles is crucial, both for our learning and for our students' learning.

In the end, we need to be familiar with our students' strengths and needs, our own comfort level, the demands of the content, and available resources. With this information in mind, we can choose which entry point works best for us and at what pace we should move.

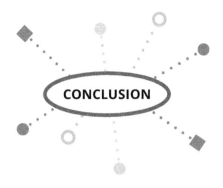

QUESTIONS. ANSWERS. ACTIONS.

If you are among those who believe that it
can't be done, then please do not interrupt this
classroom, as we are currently doing it.
— CHINESE PROVERB (MODIFIED)

SUCCESSFUL CHANGE STARTS with the first step. Celebrating this first step is key to our future success. When trying something new, many of us focus on what went wrong. While this focus can help us grow, our brains and psyche also require positive reinforcement. If we ignore what went right and instead focus only on the negative, we are not giving ourselves the kind of feedback we need. In fact, we are likely reinforcing negative practices. Don't be afraid to pause and celebrate the successes you experience.

In their book *Switch*, Chip and Dan Heath remind us that successful change requires direction, motivation, and a plan. You know your direction: project based learning. You know your motivation: quality student learning. And now, hopefully, you have a plan.

We occasionally hear educators make comments such as, "We're going to make this unit a PBL," or, "This year, it's my goal to do two PBLs." While starting small and setting an attainable goal can help to initiate something new, be careful about creating a fierce dichotomy between your class with PBL and your class without PBL. The truth is, for project based learning to yield successful results, it can't be approached like a light bulb: on one day, off the next. And, it most certainly shouldn't be used as the occasional "special learning" stuck in the middle of more traditional practices. These abrupt on-again, off-again tendencies send mixed messages to students regarding how they should learn. They interrupt the development of routines, and they ultimately hurt our ability to create sustainable change. Infusing PBL-supportive practices, detailed throughout this book, should be the goal, regardless of whether or not "full-blown" project based learning is taking place. We can create classes that are always brimming with positive relationships, inquiry, student talk, and more. Remember, culture isn't built overnight; it requires consistent attention and care.

A DIRECT CORRELATION EXISTS BETWEEN THE NUMBER OF RISKS WE TAKE AND THE NUMBER OF CRITICISMS WE'RE LIKELY TO FACE.

A direct correlation exists between the number of risks we take and the number of criticisms we're likely to face. Simply put, when we teach differently, others may denounce what they don't understand (trust us, we know). While it's certainly easier said than done, we need to do what we can to drown out the voices of detractors in favor of what's best for our students. In *Daring Greatly* (2012),

Brené Brown gets to the heart of this idea: "Nothing has transformed my life more than realizing that it's a waste of time to evaluate my worthiness by weighing the reaction of the people in the stands." We must evaluate ourselves based on the work of our students, not the pushback from our critics. All great educators have at least this in common: They keep students at the center of their work, and they advocate for them accordingly.

Finally, if we're waiting around for the perfect time, perfect idea, or perfect answer, we'll never get started with project based learning, or we'll never take this work further. The tricky thing about answers is that there are never enough of them, and answers tend to elicit more and more questions. What we have is a vicious yet beautiful cycle of questions and answers. When we decide to embrace this cycle, our only option is to propel forward and learn, for ourselves and for our students. And, at certain points throughout this learning, we gain the courage to take the knowledge and skills we've acquired and put them into action. This is when all of our hard work pays off.

REAL QUESTIONS. REAL ANSWERS.

We encourage you to keep learning and keep asking questions. Most of all, we hope you will feel inspired to share some answers of your own.

Additional resources are available on the book's website: realpbl.com. Our Facebook group, which includes thousands of like-minded members, can be found at facebook.com/groups/realpbl. When joining the discussion online, please use the hashtag #RealPBL.

We would love to connect with you on your journey.

About the Authors

Ross Cooper

As a nationally recognized leader in project based learning, Ross has worked with thousands of educators across the country to implement PBL, and in 2016, he coauthored *Hacking Project Based Learning: 10 Easy Steps to PBL and Inquiry in the Classroom*. While his day job is his first professional priority, he finds time to conduct workshops and speak on project based learning, inquiry-based learning, student-centered learning, instructional leadership, his professional experiences, and more. Ross is currently an administrator in the Chappaqua Central School District in New York. Previously, he was an elementary school principal, K–12 curriculum supervisor, elementary assistant principal, and fourth grade teacher. He is an Apple Distinguished Educator and a Google Certified Innovator. When he is not working, he enjoys eating steak and pizza and provoking his four beautiful nephews and niece. He blogs at RossCoops31.com, and you can connect with him via email, RossCoops31@gmail.com, and on Twitter @RossCoops31.

Erin Murphy

Erin consults internationally with leaders and learners regarding literacy, learning, and leadership, and is coauthor of *Hacking Project Based Learning: 10 Easy Steps to PBL and Inquiry in the Classroom* (2016). She currently has the pleasure of serving as the supervisor of teaching and learning for the humanities subjects in the East Penn School District in Pennsylvania.

She spent four years as a middle school assistant principal and has classroom experiences ranging from kindergarten through fifth grade. She is a proud graduate of Penn State University's Professional Development School, where she was trained in inquiry-based instructional approaches. Erin, her husband, and their two daughters reside in Pennsylvania, and the family enjoys spending time gardening, watching football, and playing board games. You can connect with Erin through her blog, psumurphette.com, via email at psumurphette@gmail.com, and on Twitter @MurphysMusings5.

Acknowledgments

Ross

Once again, I first and foremost would like to thank my father, Melvin Charles Cooper, for working tirelessly and endlessly to ensure a quality life for our family. To my mother, Judith Cooper, thank you for helping to raise me. To my siblings—Spencer, Whitney, and Craig—thank you for always being by my side. To the handful of professional colleagues who have truly helped to shape who I am as an educator and person: Anthony Moyer, Kristen Campbell, Tony Sinanis, Tom Murray, and Nancy Gambuti. Together, we are better. Of course, I also owe a great deal to the administrators, teachers, students, and families of my current employer, Chappaqua Central School District.

Erin

Thank you to my colleagues in the East Penn School District. For the last thirteen years, I have had the honor and privilege to serve East Penn, and I continue to have opportunities to grow as an educator. For that I am forever grateful. To my parents, Rose and Bill Hamilton, for teaching me the importance of education and hard work. To my daughters for serving as my inspiration to be good and do good; I love you to the moon and back. To my husband, Nate, for his endless support and honesty. Thank you for keeping me fed, caffeinated, and loved. None of this would be possible without you.

APPENDIX:

Where Can I Find More?

The following free resources, and more, can be found at realpbl.com.

Templates

A blank project planning template and a blank Progress Assessment Tool template.

Premade Projects

We hesitate to offer premade projects, but when designing our own, we know it can help to refer to preexisting projects, in the same way that students benefit from examples. We have selected grade levels and content areas that often present the most challenge for PBL implementation: primary grades, English class, math class, and high school social studies. Even if none of these grade levels or areas apply to your work, you can still benefit from exploring the ways in which these projects are laid out.

#RealPBL Discussion Questions

30 questions to guide discussions and reflection.

PBL Paralysis Graphics

All eight graphics from the book.

Illustrations

All four graphics from the book, in color.

Posters with Pull-Quotes

Color graphics with some of our favorite quotes from the book.

eBooks

How Else Can Inquiry Happen?
Explore the connections between project based learning and design thinking, Genius Hour, personalized learning, and makerspaces.

How Do I Lead Project Based Learning?
Provides a concrete framework for leading the implementation of project based learning and other instructional shifts.

A Step-by-Step Guide to Project Based Learning in a Virtual World
Designed for remote learning, this resource makes project based learning as intuitive as possible without sacrificing what makes this learner-centered approach unique.

#RealPBL Deleted Scenes
Contains excerpts that didn't make it into the final draft of this book.

Work with Us

Discover opportunities for us to collaborate.

References

Anderson, C. (2018). *A Teacher's Guide to Writing Conferences*. Portsmouth, NH: Heinemann.

Bandura, A. (1997). *Self-Efficacy: The Exercise of Control*. New York, NY: W. H. Freeman.

Blodget, H. (2012, January 22). Steve Jobs freaked out a month before first iPhone was released and demanded a new screen. *Business Insider*. Retrieved from https://www.businessinsider.com/steve-jobs-new-iphone-screen-2012-1

Brown, B. (2012). *Daring Greatly: How the Courage to be Vulnerable Transforms the Way We Live, Love, Parent, and Lead*. New York, NY: Avery.

Bruce Mau Design. (2010). *The Third Teacher: 79 Ways You Can Use Design to Transform Teaching & Learning*. New York, NY: Abrams.

Calkins, L. (1994). *The Art of Teaching Writing*. Portsmouth, NH: Heinemann.

Catmull, E., & Wallace, A. (2014). *Creativity, Inc.: Overcoming the Unseen Forces that Stand in the Way of True Inspiration*. New York, NY: Random House.

Chui, M., & Manyika, J. (2015). Four Fundamentals of Workplace Automation. *McKinsey Quarterly*. Retrieved from https://www.mckinsey.com/business-functions/mckinsey-digital/our-insights/four-fundamentals-of-workplace-automation

Cooper, R., & Murphy, E. (2018). *Hacking Project Based Learning: 10 Easy Steps to PBL and Inquiry in the Classroom*. Highland Heights, OH: Times 10 Publications.

Covey, S. (2004). *The 7 Habits of Highly Effective People: Powerful Lessons in Personal Change*. New York, NY: Simon & Schuster.

Dillon, R., & Hare, R. (2016). *The Space: A Guide for Educators*. Irvine, CA: EdTechTeam Press.

Doorley, S., & Witthoft, S. (2012). *Make Space: How to Set the Stage for Creative Collaboration*. Hoboken, NJ: John Wiley & Sons.

Dweck, C. (2016). *Mindset: The New Psychology of Success*. New York, NY: Random House.

Fang, S., & Logonnathan, L. (2016). *Assessment for Learning Within and Beyond the Classroom: Taylor's 8th teaching and learning conference 2015 proceedings*. New York, NY: Springer.

Fisher, A., Godwin, K., & Seltman, H. (2014). Visual Environment, Attention Allocation, and Learning in Young Children: When Too Much of a Good Thing May Be Bad. *Psychological Science, 25*(7), 1362–1370.

Hattie, J. (2012). *Visible Learning for Teachers: Maximizing Impact on Learning*. New York, NY: Routledge.

Heath, C., & Heath, D. (2010). *Switch: How to Change Things When Change Is Hard*. New York, NY: Broadway Books.

Hess, K. (2018). *A Local Assessment Toolkit to Promote Deeper Learning: Transforming Research Into Practice*. Thousand Oaks, CA: Corwin.

Hodges, T. (2018). Not Just a Buzzword. *Principal, 98*(1), 10–13.

Kelley, T., & Kelley, D. (2013). *Creative Confidence: Unleashing the Creative Potential Within Us All*. New York, NY: Crown Business.

Kleon, A. (2012). Steal Like an Artist: 10 Things Nobody Told You About Being Creative. New York, NY: Workman.

Kohn, A. (September 2001). Five Reasons to Stop Saying "Good Job!" [Blog post]. Retrieved from https://www.alfiekohn.org/article/five-reasons-stop-saying-good-job/

Kohn, A. (2011). The Case Against Grades. *Educational Leadership, 69*(3), 28–33.

Kotter, J. (2012). *Leading Change*. Boston, MA: Harvard Business Review Press.

Larmer, J., Mergendoller, J., & Boss, S. (2015). *Setting the Standard for Project Based Learning: A Proven Approach to Rigorous Classroom Instruction*. Alexandria, VA: ASCD.

Lencioni, P. (2002). *The Five Dysfunctions of a Team: A Leadership Fable*. San Francisco, CA: Jossey-Bass.

McNair, A. (2017). *Genius Hour: Passion Projects that Ignite Innovation and Student Inquiry*. Waco, TX: Prufrock Press Inc.

McTighe, J., & Wiggins, G. (2015). *Solving 25 Problems in Unit Design: How Do I Refine My Units to Enhance Student Learning?* Alexandria, VA: ASCD.

Meyer, D. (2012, August 9). Khan Academy Does Angry Birds [Blog post]. Retrieved from https://blog.mrmeyer.com/2012/khan-academy-does-angry-birds

Nair, P. (2014). *Blueprint for Tomorrow: Redesigning Schools for Student-Centered Learning*. Cambridge, MA: Harvard Education Press.

National Association of Colleges and Employers. (2020). Job Outlook 2020. Retrieved from https://www.vidteamcc.com/ stadistics/2020-nace-job-outlook%20(1).pdf

Organization for Economic Cooperation and Development. Futures Thinking In brief. Retrieved from https://www.oecd.org/ site/schoolingfortomorrowknowledgebase/futuresthinking/futur-esthinkinginbrief.htm

PBLWorks. (2019). Collaboration Rubric for PBL: Individual Performance for Grades 3–5; Common Core ELA aligned. Retrieved from https://my.pblworks.org/system/files/documents/ PBLWorks-3-5-Collaboration-Rubric-CCSS.pdf

Pierson, R. (2013, May). *Rita Pierson: Every Kid Needs a Champion* [Video file]. Retrieved from https://www.ted.com/talks/ rita_pierson_every_kid_needs_a_champion

Pink, D. (2009, July). *Dan Pink: The Puzzle of Motivation* [Video file]. Retrieved from https://www.ted.com/talks/dan_pink_on_motivation

Port, M. (2015). *Steal the Show: From Speeches to Job Interviews to Deal-Closing Pitches, How to Guarantee a Standing Ovation for All the Performances In Your Life.* New York, NY: Houghton Mifflin Harcourt.

Quaglia Institute for School Voice and Aspirations. (2016). School Voice Report 2016. Retrieved from http://quagliainstitute.org/ dmsView/School_Voice_Report_2016

Quinn, T. (2012, December 7). G-R-O-U-P W-O-R-K Doesn't Spell Collaboration. *Education Week*. Retrieved from https:// www.edweek.org/ew/articles/2012/12/01/kappan_quinn.html

Ray, K. W., & Laminack, L. (2001). *The Writing Workshop: Working Through the Hard Parts (and They're All Hard Parts).* Urbana, IL: National Council of Teachers of English.

Reeves, D. (2010). *Transforming Professional Development Into Student Results.* Alexandria, VA: ASCD.

Ritchhart, R., Church, M., & Morrison, K. (2011). *Making Thinking Visible: How to Promote Engagement, Understanding, and Independence for All Learners.* San Francisco, CA: Jossey-Bass.

Rothstein, D., & Santana, L. (2011). *Make Just One Change: Teach Students to Ask Their Own Questions.* Cambridge, MA: Harvard Education Press.

Sackstein, S. (2017). *Peer Feedback in the Classroom: Empowering Students to Be the Experts.* Alexandria, VA: ASCD.

Schmoker, M. (2011). *Focus: Elevating the Essentials to Radically Improve Student Learning.* Alexandria, VA: ASCD.

Spencer, J., & Juliani, A. J. (2016). *LAUNCH: Using Design Thinking to Boost Creativity and Bring Out the Maker in Every Student.* San Diego, CA: Dave Burgess Consulting, Inc.

Stone, D., & Heen, S. (2014). *Thanks for the Feedback: The Science and Art of Receiving Feedback Well.* New York, NY: Penguin Books.

TEDx Talks. (2011, March). *Alan November* [Video file]. Retrieved from https://www.youtube.com/watch?v=ebJHzpEy4bE

Thornburg, D. (1999). *Campfires in Cyberspace.* Lake Barrington, IL: Starsong.

Tomlinson, C. A. (2017). *How to Differentiate Instruction in Academically Diverse Classrooms* (3rd ed.). Alexandria, VA: ASCD.

Van de Walle, J. (1999). *Reform Mathematics vs. the Basics: Understanding the Conflict and Dealing with It.* Retrieved from http://www.mathematically-sane.com

Van de Walle, J., Karp, K., Lovin, L. A., & Bay-Williams, J. (2018). *Teaching Student-Centered Mathematics: Developmentally Appropriate Instruction for Grades 3–5.* Upper Saddle River, NJ: Pearson.

Watkins, M. (2012). *The First 90 Days: Proven Strategies for Getting Up to Speed Faster and Smarter.* Boston, MA: Harvard Business Review Press.

Wiggins, G. (2012). Seven Keys to Effective Feedback. *Educational Leadership, 70*(1), 10–16.

Wiggins, G. (2014, August 30). UbD and Inquiry – A Response to 2 Questions [Blog post]. Retrieved from https://grantwiggins.wordpress.com/2014/08/30/ubd-and-inquiry-a-response-to-2-questions

Wiggins, G., & McTighe, J. (2005). *Understanding by Design.* Alexandria, VA: ASCD.

Wormeli, R. (2018). *Fair Isn't Always Equal: Assessment and Grading in the Differentiated Classroom.* Portland, ME: Stenhouse.

Wujec, T. (2010, February). *Tom Wujec: Build a Tower, Build a Team* [Video file]. Retrieved from https://www.ted.com/talks/tom_wujec_build_a_tower

More from Times 10

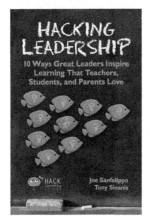

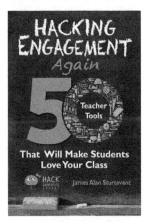

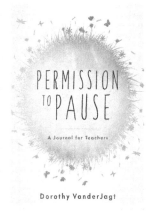

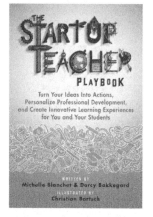

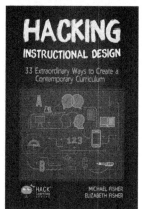

Resources from Times 10

10Publications.com

**Join the Times 10 Ambassadors
and help us revolutionize education:**
10Publications.com/ambassador

Podcasts:
hacklearningpodcast.com
jamesalansturtevant.com/podcast

On Twitter:
@10Publications
@HackMyLearning
#Times10News
#RealPBL
@LeadForward2
#LeadForward
#HackLearning
#HackingLeadership
#MakeWriting
#HackingQs
#HackingSchoolDiscipline
#LeadWithGrace
#QuietKidsCount
#ModernMentor
#AnxiousBook

All things Times 10:
10Publications.com

10PUBLICATIONS.COM

Times 10 provides practical solutions that busy educators can read today and use tomorrow. We bring you content from experts, shared through books, podcasts, and an array of social networks. Our books bring Vision, Experience, and Action to educators around the world. Stay in touch with us at 10Publications. com and follow our updates on Twitter @10Publications and #Times10News.

Made in the USA
Middletown, DE
25 May 2021